FAMILY LIFE
HOMEBUILDERS
COUPLES SERIES®

GROWING TOGETHER IN CHRIST

BIBLE STUDY ELECTIVE

"Unless the Lord builds the house,
they labor in vain who build it."
Psalm 127:1

DAVID SUNDE

Dennis Rainey, Senior Editor

Gospel Light

How to Let The Lord Build Your House
AND NOT LABOR IN VAIN

FamilyLife is a part of Campus Crusade for Christ International, an evangelical Christian organization founded in 1951 by Bill Bright. FamilyLife was started in 1976 to help fulfill the Great Commission by strengthening marriages and families and then equipping them to go to the world with the gospel of Jesus Christ. Our FamilyLife Marriage Conference is held in most major cities throughout the United States and is one of the fastest-growing marriage conferences in America today. Information on all resources offered by FamilyLife may be obtained by either writing or calling us at the address and telephone number listed below.

PUBLISHING STAFF
William T. Greig, Publisher
Dr. Elmer L. Towns, Senior Consulting Publisher
Dr. Gary S. Greig, Senior Consulting Editor
Wes Haystead, Editor
Jean Daly, Managing Editor
Pam Weston, Editorial Assistant
Kyle Duncan, Associate Publisher
Bayard Taylor, M.Div., Editor, Theological and Biblical Issues
Debi Thayer, Designer

Growing Together in Christ Bible Study Elective
ISBN 0-8307-1816-8

Dennis Rainey, Executive Director
FamilyLife • P.O. Box 23840 • Little Rock, AR 72221-3840 • (501) 223-8663

A Ministry of Campus Crusade for Christ International
Bill Bright, Founder and President
Published by Gospel Light, Ventura, California 93003

How to Make Clean Copies from This Book

You may make copies of portions of this book with a clean conscience if:

- you (or someone in your organization) are the original purchaser;
- you are using the copies you make for a noncommercial purpose (such as teaching or promoting your ministry) within your church or organization;
- you follow the instructions provided in this book.

However, it is ILLEGAL for you to make copies if:

- you are using the material to promote, advertise or sell a product or service other than for ministry fund-raising;
- you are using the material in or on a product for sale;
- you or your organization are not the original purchaser of this book.

By following these guidelines you help us keep our products affordable.

Thank you,

Gospel Light

CONTENTS

Session 1

Obstacles to Growth as a Couple 28

All couples face barriers to growth in their Christian lives.

Session 2

Essentials for Growth as a Couple 43

The Christian life is one of exciting growth as you establish a
solid relationship with Christ.

Session 3

The Benefits of Prayer in Marriage 54

Prayer promotes growth both in your relationship with God
and in your relationship with your mate.

Session 4

The Power of Prayer in Marriage 65

Effective prayer includes praise, confession and supplication.

Session 5

The Guidebook for Growth 78

The greatest book ever written is God's gift to help you grow
closer to Him and to your mate.

Session 6

Using Your Guidebook 91

A workable plan for exploring God's Word as a couple will
help you grow closer to Him and to your mate.

Session 7

The Holy Spirit: Your Partner in Marriage 102

The Holy Spirit is available to enable any Christian couple
to experience God's best within their marriage.

ACKNOWLEDGMENTS

A vision for this HomeBuilders study was born in my heart over 15 years ago when FamilyLife was just getting underway. As Dennis Rainey and I talked then, we recognized that a firm grasp of how to live the Christian life is absolutely key to the success of any marriage. We can predict great success for a marriage when there is sound, practical knowledge of both the Creator's design and His power to lead the marriage into the highest halls of human happiness. So in 1988, when plans started coming together under Dennis Rainey's leadership, I felt a deep gratitude to him and the FamilyLife team.

Thank you, Dennis, for your perseverance to see the vision become reality. You and Barbara are models of what it means to grow together in Christ in the years of your marriage.

It is a great honor and joy to work with the FamilyLife team. From the rough sketches of our ideas and outlines to the final copy, Dave Boehi and Julie Denker have been truly indispensable.

Dave's creative gifts ensured that we were expressing our thoughts in the most effective manner. His major editing work defined for me the pursuit of excellence.

Julie's warm encouragement, faithful coordination of the production and tenacity with the deadlines kept us moving in the right direction. Thank you, Dave and Julie. I could not have done this without you.

I want to extend a very special word of thanks to the couples who met together in communities across America to field-test this study in its formative days. Your feedback and insights gave us invaluable counsel in revising the material.

To my lifetime companion, my wife Sande, a heartfelt thanks for working with me in testing the teachings of this study in the years of our marriage. By His grace, we have grown together in Christ.

FOREWORD

One of the most dangerous assumptions a Christian could ever make is that spiritual growth will just happen. Far too many Christians today become stale and stagnant because they assume that growth will occur just because they are involved in religious activities, but the New Testament teaches that spiritual growth is the result of some basic and fundamental steps that each of us as Christians are responsible to take.

Dave Sunde has been a personal friend of mine for the past 20 years, and he is no newcomer to this subject of spiritual growth. He not only brings over 30 years of experience in biblical teaching to this subject, but he also shows a rock-solid walk with Christ in his own life. In the following 12 sessions you will find that he captures the simple but profound essence of spiritual growth.

As in other studies in the **HomeBuilders Couples Series®**, Dave eloquently demonstrates that spiritual growth best occurs as we are accountable to one another—to our mates. I am thrilled that he has put these truths together in such a way that married couples who work through this study will be challenged to grow deeper in Christ.

Dennis Rainey
Executive Director of FamilyLife

INTRODUCTION

ABOUT THE HOMEBUILDERS COUPLES SERIES®

What is the purpose of the HomeBuilders Series?

Do you remember the first time you fell in love? That junior high—or elementary school—"crush" stirred your affections with little or no effort on your part. We use the term "falling in love" to describe the phenomenon of suddenly discovering our emotions have been captured by someone delightful.

Unfortunately, our society tends to make us think that all loving relationships should be equally as effortless. Thus, millions of couples, Christians included, approach their marriages certain that the emotions they feel will carry them through any difficulties. And millions of couples quickly learn that a good marriage does not automatically happen.

Otherwise intelligent people, who would not think of buying a car, investing money or even going to the grocery store without some initial planning, enter into marriage with no plan of how to make their marriage succeed.

But God has already provided the plan, a set of blueprints for a truly godly marriage. His plan is designed to enable two people to grow together in a mutually satisfying relationship, and then to look beyond their own marriage to others. Ignoring this plan leads to isolation and separation between husband and wife—the pattern so evident in the majority of homes today. Even when great energy is expended, failure to follow God's blueprints results in wasted effort, bitter disappointment—and, in far too many cases, divorce.

In response to this need in marriages today, FamilyLife of Campus Crusade for Christ created a popular series of small-group Bible studies for couples called the **HomeBuilders Couples Series®**. The series has now been adapted for larger groups so that you can lead a class of adults in a study designed to answer one question for couples:

How do you build a distinctively Christian marriage?

It is our hope that in answering this question with the biblical blueprints for building a home, we will see the development of growing, thriving marriages filled with the love of Jesus Christ.

FamilyLife is committed to strengthening your family. We hope the **HomeBuilders Couples Series®** will assist you and your church as it equips couples in building godly homes.

What is this study intended to accomplish?

Couples who participate in these sessions will find that the experience:

- Stimulates them to examine what Scripture says about how to construct a solid, satisfying marriage.
- Allows them to interact with each other on a regular basis about significant issues in their marriages.
- Encourages them to interact with other couples, establishing mutual accountability for growth efforts.
- Motivates them to take specific actions which have been valuable to couples desiring to build stronger homes.
- Creates accountability to others for growth in their marriages.

Why is accountability so important?

Accountability is a scriptural principle that tells us to "be subject to one another in the fear of Christ" (Ephesians 5:21). This means I choose to submit my life to the scrutiny of another person in order to gain spiritual strength, growth and balance.

Accountability means asking another person for advice. It means giving him or her the freedom to make honest observations and evaluations about you. It means you're teachable and approachable. True accountability involves letting another person into the interior of your life.

Adult classes which use a HomeBuilders Couples study are opening themselves up for at least a small measure of accountability. Our experience has shown that many class members will make commitments to apply aspects of the studies to their lives, but will never follow through on those commitments. As a leader, establishing an environment of friendly accountability can help your class members get the most out of this study.

Look for some hints on establishing accountability in the "How to Lead a HomeBuilders Bible Study Elective" section.

What impact has the HomeBuilders Couples Series® had in marriages?

Since we published the first HomeBuilders study in 1987, we've continually heard stories about couples whose marriages were revitalized and, in some cases, even saved. Here are some examples:

> "We started our HomeBuilders group as a follow-up to the Video FamilyLife Conference presented at our church. We have developed a good openness among the group members. It has brought problem areas to the surface and given us a greater sense of awareness of our responsibility toward our mate. One couple travels as far as an hour to attend!"
>
> Pastor, Washington

"We're using *Building Your Marriage* and *Mastering Your Money in Marriage* in our Sunday school classes, both for newlyweds and as a marriage renewal class. I have seen couples open communication lines for the first time in a long time as a result of their involvement."

> Bill Willits
> Minister to Married Adults
> First Baptist Church
> Atlanta, Ga.

"We've led three studies now, and in each one of those we have seen ourselves grow. You really do co-learn."

> Doug Grimm
> Playa Del Rey, Calif.

"I've built my family ministry around the FamilyLife Conference and the HomeBuilders. It makes biblically-minded, servant-minded people who are useful for advancing the kingdom and leadership of the kingdom."

> Jeff Rhodes, pastor
> First Presbyterian Church
> Winterhaven, Fla.

"Nine weeks of the HomeBuilders class turned everything around in our relationship. It was a real miracle. The walls came down and the masks came off. We were able to discuss matters we had swept under the carpet years ago that our enemy was consistently using to destroy the love God had designed for us since the beginning of time....

"The HomeBuilders class really works. Here is why: HomeBuilders not only shows you why, and tells you how, it teaches a way to alter your life-style so these great truths become a part of everyday living.

"We have truly overcome isolation and are building toward oneness in our marriage. We have learned how to yield to God and the leading of His Holy Spirit instead of our own selfish desires...the romance is back and the intimacy is growing every day. HomeBuilders has really given us the 'wisdom' we were looking for in our marriage.

"It is absolutely the best thing that has ever happened to us since becoming Christians 18 years ago. It changed our lives at a time I was just ready to accept apathy for parts of my marriage, figuring there was no way to ever change."

> Alan and Lanette Hauge
> Playa Del Rey, Calif.

How does this study fit into a strategy for building Christian marriages?

While this study has great value in itself, it is only the first step in a long-term process of growth. If people complete these sessions and then gradually return to their previous patterns of living, little or no good will result. Continued effort is required for people to initiate and maintain new directions in their marriages.

It is our belief, also, that no couple can truly build a Christian home and marriage without a strong commitment and involvement in a local church. The church provides the daily spiritual direction and equipping necessary for a truly godly marriage.

FamilyLife is committed to changing the destiny of the family and providing quality resources to churches and individuals to build distinctively Christian marriages. In addition to the **HomeBuilders Couples Series®**, we offer:

- "FamilyLife Today," our daily radio show with Dennis Rainey. This half-hour broadcast offers biblical, practical tips for building your family with a foundation in Christ.
- The FamilyLife Marriage Conference, a weekend getaway for couples to learn how to experience oneness in their marriages.
- The FamilyLife Parenting Conference, in which parents learn practical ways to raise their children to know and love the Lord.
- The Urban Family Conference, a shorter version of the FamilyLife Marriage Conference that is geared to the needs of African-American families.
- Numerous materials to help you grow as a family and reach out to others.

HOW TO LEAD A HOMEBUILDERS
BIBLE STUDY ELECTIVE

What It Takes to Lead a HomeBuilders Study

You may find that a HomeBuilders study is a bit different from other adult church curriculum you've used. To be specific, *small-group interaction is the foundation for the curriculum.* As class leader you take on the role of "facilitator"—a directive guide who encourages people to think, to discover what Scripture says and to interact with others in the group. The design of these sessions does not call for you to be an authority or a teacher—your job is to help the group members glean biblical truth and apply it to their lives.

In guiding the active participation of your class members, you don't want to let them ramble aimlessly or pool their ignorance. You'll need to familiarize yourself with the material so that you know where the discussion is headed and so you can provide answers when needed. The directions in this leader's guide will help you keep each session moving.

Since this is a series for couples, it will be beneficial for you and your mate to work together to make the course a success. Commit to each other and to God that this study will be a major priority for both of you.

SPECIAL NOTE ABOUT GROUP SIZE: We recommend that a group have no more than 16 people; anything larger begins to inhibit good small-group interaction. If you have a large class, we strongly urge you to divide it into smaller groups for this series and recruit leaders to guide each group. (Each group leader will need his or her own Leader's Guide.)

Using the Leader's Guide

This book and the suggestions we make are designed to cause your creative juices to flow, not cramp your style. You will undoubtedly come up with some distinctive ways to use this material. That's fine. Don't let these recommendations force you into a box.

If, however, you find it difficult to be creative as a leader, this guide will relieve your fears. In it you will find ideas, questions and tips that will help keep the study moving.

Each of the 12 sessions in this study contains the following material, in order:

Leader's Notes: This opening section includes detailed instructions and tips for the leader. Answers to questions as well as leader *Tips, Notes* and *Comments* appear in italics to distinguish them from the regular content and questions.

Student Notes: These reproducible pages include all the session questions and are handed out to group members at the beginning of each class. Notes for each session end with a **HomeBuilders Project** for group members to complete before you meet again.

Format for Each Session

The following outline gives a quick look at how the sessions are structured:

FOCUS: a statement of the overall focus of the session you will be studying.

WARM UP: a time to help people get to know each other, review the past session and begin the new study.

BLUEPRINTS: the biblical content of the session.

HOMEBUILDERS PRINCIPLES: summary points made throughout the study.

MAKE A DATE: a time for couples to decide when they will complete their HomeBuilders Project.

HOMEBUILDERS PROJECT: a 20-30 minute project to be completed at home before the next session.

RECOMMENDED READING: suggestions for use of several books to get maximum value from the study.

Although this format varies slightly from session to session, you should familiarize yourself with it so that you are aware of the purpose of each segment of the study. Explaining the segments to your class will also aid them in understanding the session's content.

Time Schedule

The time for the actual study is 45-60 minutes. If you have a longer time period available, you will be able to move at a more relaxed pace through each part of the session.

As the people in your class get to know each other better through the small-group interaction, you may find it difficult to complete a session in the time allotted. It is not necessary that every question be covered, since many are intended to stimulate thought, not to result in exhaustive discussion and resolution of every issue. Be sensitive to your use of time and be careful not to make comments about time pressure which will make the group feel rushed. For example:

- When you need to move the discussion to the next item, say something like, "We could probably talk about that question the rest of the day, but let's also consider several other important questions that bear on this issue."
- When it's necessary to reduce or eliminate the time for a question or topic, simply say, "You can see that there are several more questions we could have moved on to discuss, but I felt we were making real progress, so I chose to spend some extra time on the earlier points."

You will find, as you prepare and review for each session, that some questions or sections are more relevant to your class than other portions of the study. Pace your study in such a way that those questions which must be addressed are not rushed.

You are the leader of your class and know the needs of the individual couples. But keep in mind that the Holy Spirit will have an agenda for specific couples which you may never know about. As Proverbs 16:9 says, "The mind of man plans his way, but the Lord directs his steps." Do your best to prepare and pray over the session and then leave the results to God.

Be aware of the common tendency to get embroiled in a discussion on one point, and not have time to deal with those which follow (which may be even more significant). Even if an issue is not fully resolved, encourage people to place the topic on hold and move on to the next issues. Often, resolution of a "sticky" issue does not fully take place until all facets of a topic have been considered.

If you have 60 minutes to work with, plan at least an additional 15 minutes for fellowship, 5 or 10 minutes of which may precede the study and the remainder afterwards. When you invite people to the class, tell them to plan on the total time. This reduces having people drag in late or rush off early and not get acquainted.

Also, when you announce the study, let people know that it will go for 12 sessions. People like to know how long they are committing themselves.

The shorter time period available for a Sunday School session can pose a problem in adequately dealing with all the essential concepts in a study. A few minutes digression in a 45- to 60-minute session is harder to recoup than in the longer time period available for an evening small group. Here are three options to consider as ways to ensure the best use of the limited time available:

1. *Eliminate for these sessions the normal singing, announcements and other activities which are often a part of many adult classes.* Inform class members that you intend to use the full session for learning and fellowship features which are vital to the impact of the study. People who are used to slipping in late may need an extra nudge to get them there on time. The informal fellowship dimension which is vital to helping people feel at home in the group can be done before and after the session. The leader will need to be very sensitive to using that time wisely, since people will have other commitments that keep them from lingering.

2. *If you have 60 minutes or less available, look for ways to condense parts of the actual study to about 45 minutes.* One way to accomplish this is to cut a few questions. Look through each lesson and determine what is most important to cover, and mark the questions that you think could be eliminated. Perhaps you can choose just one question from a **Warm Up** to use, for example.

3. *You can also save time by dividing your class into small groups and assigning specific questions (or verses) to different groups for discussion.* Then have representatives from the small groups report briefly to the whole class. If you have less than eight or nine couples, you could do most discussions with the class as a whole. But if your class is larger, we suggest dividing into groups of three couples each. You could either assign each couple to a permanent group throughout the entire study, or you could divide the class into different groups each session.

In working with small groups in your class, decide in advance if you want to appoint a leader in each group or if you prefer guiding the discussion from up front. If you do want to guide the discussion, you could switch back and forth between having the individuals answer questions to the whole class and answering them just within the small groups.

How the Bible Is Used in This Study

As you proceed through this study, you will notice that the Bible is regarded as the final authority on the issues of life and marriage. Although written centuries ago, this Book still speaks clearly and powerfully about the conflicts and struggles men and women face. The Bible is God's Word and contains His blueprints for building a godly home and for dealing with the practical issues of living.

While Scripture has only one primary interpretation, there may be several appropriate applications. Some of the passages used in this series were not originally written with marriage in mind, but they can be applied practically to the husband-wife relationship.

Encourage each group member to have a Bible with him or her for each session. The *New American Standard Bible*, the *New International Version®* and the *New King James Version* are three excellent English versions which make the Bible easy to understand.

Ground Rules for Each Session

These sessions are designed to be enjoyable and informative—and nonthreatening. Three simple ground rules will help ensure that everyone feels comfortable and gets the most out of the study:

1. Share nothing about your marriage which will embarrass your mate.
2. You may "pass" on any question you do not want to answer.
3. Complete the **HomeBuilders Projects** (questions for each couple to discuss and act on) between each session. Be prepared to share one result at the next group meeting.

Setting Up Your Class

You need a room where everyone can sit comfortably and see and hear each other. Avoid letting couples or individuals sit outside the group; they will not feel included. The seating arrangement is very important to discussion and involvement.

- Chairs should be easily moved to enable formation of small groups, and the room should be large enough to allow couples opportunity to talk "privately."
- Leave adequate open space where people can mingle casually before and after the session.
- Set up chairs around tables or in circles of six to eight. For variety in some sessions, you may want to set the chairs in a large semicircle (with more than one row if necessary). Avoid straight rows that leave people seeing only the backs of heads.

Plan to occasionally use a chalkboard, overhead projector or flipchart to emphasize key points, to focus attention on key questions or Scriptures and/or to write instructions for assignments to be done by individuals, couples or small groups. Be cautious about overusing these tools, as they can set a "classroom" tone which may inhibit some people from full participation.

If you want a comfortable, relaxed setting that encourages people to get to know one another, something to sip and swallow is almost essential. Depending on the time of your meeting, you may find it works well to offer both hot and cold beverages and light "munchies" (donuts, muffins, fruit slices, etc.) as people arrive. Have enough ready to also have something available at the close of the study to encourage people to continue talking with each other for a while.

People to Invite

The concepts in this study will benefit any couple, whether they are newlyweds, engaged, married many years or even just looking ahead to the possibilities of marriage. Leading the class will be easier if your group is made up of couples at generally similar stages in their relationships. The more they have in common, the easier it will be for them to identify with one another and open up in sharing.

On the other hand, it also can be helpful for a couple to gain a fresh viewpoint on marriage by interacting with a couple having significantly different experiences. In other words, if a couple is interested in building and maintaining a strong marriage, they belong in this study.

Expect some people, especially some husbands, to attend the first session wishing they were someplace else. Some will be there just because their mate or another couple nagged them to come. Some may be suspicious of a "Bible" class. Others may be fearful of revealing any weaknesses in their marriage. And some may feel either that their marriage is beyond help or that they do not need any help.

You can dispel a great deal of anxiety and resistance at the first session. Simply begin by mentioning that you know there are probably some who came reluctantly. Share a few reasons people may feel that way, and affirm that regardless of why anyone has come, you are pleased each person is there.

Briefly comment on how the concepts in this study have helped you and your marriage and express your confidence that each person will enjoy the study and benefit from it. Also, assure the group that at no time will anyone be forced to share publicly. What each person shares is his or her choice—no one will be embarrassed.

In spite of such efforts, over the course of the study, some people are likely to have to come to at least some sessions without a partner. Assure these people that you are glad they made the effort to come alone. Make sure you include them in class discussions. When having people meet as couples, consider these alternatives for those without partners:

- Have them meet with another person whose spouse is not present. Encourage them to focus on their own efforts to build their marriages, not talking about what their mates do or don't do.
- Invite them to write answers and reflections to share later with their mates.

Also, the study is definitely targeted at Christians, but many non-Christian couples have participated in it. You may find a non-Christian couple or individual who wants to build a strong marriage and is willing to participate. Welcome the non-Christian into your class and seek to get to know the person during the early sessions of the study.

Sometime during the study, schedule a time to meet with this person or couple privately to explain the principles on which this study is built. Share Christ and offer an opportunity to receive Him as Savior and Lord. We recommend "The Four Spiritual Laws" to help you explain how a person can know God. This information is included in Appendix A.

Suggestions for Guiding the Group Discussions

Keep the focus on what Scripture says, not on you or your ideas—or those of the group members, either. When someone disagrees with Scripture, affirm him or her for wrestling with the issue and point out that some biblical statements are hard to understand or to accept. Encourage the person to keep an open mind on the issue at least through the remainder of the study.

Avoid labeling an answer as "wrong"; doing so can kill the atmosphere for discussion. Encourage a person who gives an incorrect or incomplete answer to look again at the question or the Scripture being explored. Offer a comment such as, "That's really close" or "There's something else we need to see there." Or ask others in the group to respond.

Getting Everyone to Participate

A good way to encourage a nonparticipant to respond is to ask him or her to share an opinion or a personal experience rather than posing a question that can be answered yes or no or that requires a specific correct answer.

An overly talkative person can intimidate others from participating. Such behavior can be kept in control by the use of devices that call for responses in a specific manner (and which also help group members get to know little things about each other):

- "I'd like this question to be answered first by the husband of the couple with the next anniversary."
- "...the wife of the couple who had the shortest engagement."
- "...any husband who knows his mother-in-law's maiden name."
- "...anyone who complained about doing last session's project."

There are other devices for guiding responses from the class including:

- Go around the class in sequence with each person offering a one-sentence comment about a particular question without repeating what anyone else has said. If the class has more than 12 people, select one section of the class to participate in this sharing.
- Ask couples to talk with each other about a question, then ask for a show of hands of the partners who have said the least so far in this session. Then invite volunteers from those who raised their hands to report on their answers.
- Limit answers to one or two sentences—or to 30 seconds each.

Establishing an Environment of Accountability

From the outset, emphasize the importance of completing the **HomeBuilders Project** after each session. These projects give couples the opportunity to discuss what they've learned and apply it to their lives. The couples who complete these projects will get two or three times as much out of this study as will those who do not.

The most important thing you can do is state at the end of the first session that *at your next meeting you will ask each couple to share something they learned from the HomeBuilders Project.* Then, at the next session, follow through on your promise. If they know you are going to hold them accountable, they'll be more motivated to complete the projects. And they'll be glad they did!

Remember, though, to make this an environment of *friendly* accountability. You should emphasize how beneficial the projects are, and how much persons will grow in their marriage relationships if they complete them. State that you are not here to pressure or to condemn, but to help. And when you begin the following session by asking couples to tell what they learned from the project, do it with an attitude of encouragement and forgiveness. Don't seek to embarrass anyone.

One way to establish friendly accountability and to help couples know each other better is to pair up the couples in your class and assign them to be prayer partners or accountability partners. Have them call each other at some point in between class sessions to exchange prayer requests and to see if they've completed their projects.

Another possibility to consider is making a special effort to hold the men accountable to be the initiator in completing the projects. You'd need to commit yourself to calling the men in between sessions.

Another option is to divide the class into two or more teams. Each session require couples to turn in an affidavit that they completed their project. Tabulate the results. The team with the lowest completion rate must provide some agreed upon benefit (preferably edible) for the winning team at the end of the series.

HomeBuilders Principle #1:

The true Christian life is an exciting, everyday relationship with the living Christ.

HomeBuilders Principle #2:

As two people grow closer to God, they will experience greater oneness in their marriage.

HomeBuilders Principle #3:

Praying to God together helps produce the cleansing, forgiveness, humility and unity essential to continued growth in marriage.

HomeBuilders Principle #4:

The Bible gives couples a solid foundation for making moral and ethical decisions in a godless culture.

HomeBuilders Principle #5:

Couples who place a high value on knowing the Bible will discover the spiritual food their souls need to survive.

HomeBuilders Principle #6:

It is possible to become a Christian with little Bible knowledge, but it is impossible to grow together in Christ without regular study of the Scriptures.

HomeBuilders Principle #7:

The growing Christian life is the Spirit-filled life. The Holy Spirit provides the power you need to obey God on a daily basis.

HomeBuilders Principle #8:

A Christian couple will grow and experience true oneness in marriage by the presence and power of the Holy Spirit.

HomeBuilders Principle #9:

God desires that we commit our lives to following Him.

HomeBuilders Principle #10:

The benefits of following Christ easily outweigh the costs.

HomeBuilders Principle #11:

Couples who become disciples of Christ grow by showing love.

HomeBuilders Principle #12:
Couples who become disciples of Jesus Christ grow
by serving others.

HomeBuilders Principle #13:
God can use anyone who makes himself or
herself available to His call.

HomeBuilders Principle #14:
"Successful witnessing is simply sharing the gospel
in the power of the Holy Spirit and leaving the
results to God." Bill Bright

HomeBuilders Principle #15:
Growing couples who reproduce themselves spiritually
will leave an untold impact upon the next generation.

A WORD ABOUT GROWING TOGETHER

To summarize the Christian life in 12 interactive sessions is somewhat like trying to summarize the Olympic Games. A listing of the events, the competitors and the locations of the various events is essential, but there's more to the Olympics than just a dry list. The drama of athletes experiencing "the thrill of victory and the agony of defeat," the deafening roar from the stadium and the sense that history is being written make our hearts beat faster. To attend the Olympics is the privilege of a lifetime, and so is the experience of growing together in Christ.

In these 12 life-changing sessions, you'll help your class members *start* the process of growing together in Christ. The essentials are here, but the actual living out of the principles is where you and your people will experience the real adventure.

Reality ensures that you will sometimes know the agony of defeat, but let wisdom remind you not to lose heart. The thrill of victory—oneness in the spiritual dimension—will come as you learn to let go of your selfish concerns and follow Christ together.

Athletes who qualify to compete in the Olympic Games have succeeded in meeting the high standards of their events and mastering the required disciplines. In a similar way, as you grow together in spiritual oneness, you will be answering the high call of following Christ. In these sessions you will be introduced to the necessary disciplines.

But that is not the whole story. At the heart of growing together in the Lord is the incredible joy of actually coming to know God in a personal way. He has opened the way for us through Jesus Christ! I invite you and the couples in your class to enjoy Him, even as countless couples, who are now in the heavenly stadium cheering us on to victory, have.

David Sunde

INTRODUCTION

ABOUT THE HOMEBUILDERS COUPLES SERIES®

What is the purpose of the HomeBuilders Series?

Do you remember the first time you fell in love? That junior high—or elementary school—"crush" stirred your affections with little or no effort on your part. We use the term "falling in love" to describe the phenomenon of suddenly discovering our emotions have been captured by someone delightful.

Unfortunately, our society tends to make us think that all loving relationships should be equally as effortless. Thus, millions of couples, Christians included, approach their marriages certain that the emotions they feel will carry them through any difficulties. And millions of couples quickly learn that a good marriage does not automatically happen.

Otherwise intelligent people, who would not think of buying a car, investing money or even going to the grocery store without some initial planning, enter into marriage with no plan of how to make their marriage succeed.

But God has already provided the plan, a set of blueprints for a truly godly marriage. His plan is designed to enable two people to grow together in a mutually satisfying relationship, and then to look beyond their own marriage to others. Ignoring this plan leads to isolation and separation between husband and wife—the pattern so evident in the majority of homes today. Even when great energy is expended, failure to follow God's blueprints results in wasted effort, bitter disappointment—and, in far too many cases, divorce.

In response to this need in marriages today, FamilyLife of Campus Crusade for Christ created a popular series of small-group Bible studies for couples called the **HomeBuilders Couples Series®**. The series has now been adapted for larger groups such as adult Sunday School classes.

How do you build a distinctively Christian marriage?

It is our hope that in answering this question with the biblical blueprints for building a home, we will see the development of growing, thriving marriages filled with the love of Jesus Christ.

FamilyLife is committed to strengthening your family. We hope the **HomeBuilders Couples Series®** will assist you and your church as it equips couples in building godly homes.

How the Bible Is used in this study

As you proceed through this study, you will notice that the Bible is regarded as the final authority on the issues of life and marriage. Although written centuries ago, this Book still speaks clearly and powerfully about the conflicts and struggles men and women face. The Bible is God's Word and contains His blueprints for building a godly home and for dealing with the practical issues of living.

While Scripture has only one primary interpretation, there may be several appropriate applications. Some of the passages used in this series were not originally written with marriage in mind, but they can be applied practically to the husband-wife relationship.

Each group member is encouraged to have a Bible with him or her for each session. The *New American Standard Bible*, the *New International Version*® and the *New King James Version* are three excellent English versions which make the Bible easy to understand.

Ground Rules for Each Session

These sessions are designed to be enjoyable and informative—and nonthreatening. Three simple ground rules will help ensure that everyone feels comfortable and gets the most out of the study:

1. Share nothing about your marriage which will embarrass your mate.
2. You may "pass" on any question you do not want to answer.
3. Complete the **HomeBuilders Projects** (questions for each couple to discuss and act on) between each session. Be prepared to share one result at the next group meeting.

HomeBuilders Principle #1:

The true Christian life is an exciting, everyday relationship with the living Christ.

HomeBuilders Principle #2:

As two people grow closer to God, they will experience greater oneness in their marriage.

HomeBuilders Principle #3:

Praying to God together helps produce the cleansing, forgiveness, humility and unity essential to continued growth in marriage.

HomeBuilders Principle #4:

The Bible gives couples a solid foundation for making moral and ethical decisions in a godless culture.

HomeBuilders Principle #5:

Couples who place a high value on knowing the Bible will discover the spiritual food their souls need to survive.

HomeBuilders Principle #6:

It is possible to become a Christian with little Bible knowledge, but it is impossible to grow together in Christ without regular study of the Scriptures.

HomeBuilders Principle #7:

The growing Christian life is the Spirit-filled life. The Holy Spirit provides the power you need to obey God on a daily basis.

HomeBuilders Principle #8:

A Christian couple will grow and experience true oneness in marriage by the presence and power of the Holy Spirit.

HomeBuilders Principle #9:

God desires that we commit our lives to following Him.

HomeBuilders Principle #10:

The benefits of following Christ easily outweigh the costs.

HomeBuilders Principle #11:

Couples who become disciples of Christ grow by showing love.

HomeBuilders Principle #12:
Couples who become disciples of Jesus Christ
grow by serving others.

HomeBuilders Principle #13:
God can use anyone who makes himself or
herself available to His call.

HomeBuilders Principle #14:
"Successful witnessing is simply sharing the gospel
in the power of the Holy Spirit and leaving the
results to God." Bill Bright

HomeBuilders Principle #15:
Growing couples who reproduce themselves spiritually
will leave an untold impact upon the next generation.

Obstacles to Growth as a Couple

OBJECTIVES

You will help your group members start building a foundation for Christian growth as you guide them to:

- Discover that a Christian can grow in his or her faith just as a person matures in physical growth; and
- Understand what prevents some Christians from growing spiritually.

COMMENTS

Every couple faces a variety of obstacles which hinder their growing together in Christ. The theme and focus of our study in Session One is not to bemoan the difficulties nor to excuse a lack of growth. Our purpose is to raise awareness that growth will not come automatically, but only as the result of a shared desire and commitment.

STARTING THE FIRST SESSION

1. Duplicate copies of the Session One reproducible handouts for each individual in the class. You will also want to have Bibles and extra pens or pencils for class members who may have forgotten to bring their own. Option: Personally distribute the introductory pages during the week before this first session to lay the groundwork for the study.
2. Welcome group members individually as they arrive. Introduce those who do not know each other and assist them in beginning some informal conversation. Name tags will help couples get to know one another. A choice of hot or cold beverages and a light refreshment will help people relax and begin to anticipate an enjoyable time together.

3. Start the session on time, even if everyone is not yet present. Briefly share a few positive feelings about leading this study:

   - Express your interest in strengthening your own marriage and your own Christian walk.
   - Admit that your marriage is not perfect, nor have you "arrived" in terms of your Christian journey.
   - State that the concepts in this study have been helpful in your marriage and your life as a Christian.
   - Recognize that various individuals or couples may have been reluctant to come (pressured by a spouse or friend, wary of a "Christian" group, sensitive about problems with marriage and/or life, stress in schedule which makes it difficult to set aside the time for this series, etc.).
   - Thank group members for their interest and willingness to participate.

4. Hand out copies of the student introductory article "About the **HomeBuilders Couples Series®**" if you have not already done so. Give a quick overview of the series and this study. Briskly point out three or four topics and the benefits of studying them. Don't be afraid to do a little selling here; people need to know how they are personally going to benefit. They also need to know where this study will take them, especially if they are even a little bit apprehensive about the group. Explain the format for each session in no more than two or three minutes, using Session One as your example. Each session contains the following components:

   Focus—a capsule statement of the main point of the session.

   Warm Up—a time to get better acquainted with each other and to begin thinking of the session topic.

   Blueprints—discovering God's purposes and plans for marriage.

   HomeBuilders Principles—summary points made throughout the study.

   Make a Date—a time to decide when during the week they will complete the **HomeBuilders Project**.

   HomeBuilders Project—half an hour during the week when husband and wife interact with the implications of what was learned. These times are really the heart of the series.

   Recommended Reading—books that couples can read together to get maximum benefit from the study.

5. Then call attention to the ground rules for the sessions which are printed in the introductory pages.

Note: In the instructions which follow, material that appears in the handouts is presented in regular type. Added material for the leader appears in italics.

All couples face barriers to growth in
their Christian lives.

*Students are on
page 37.*

(15-20 Minutes)

*The Warm Up is intended to set a friendly, enjoyable tone from the beginning. Even if your
group is already well acquainted, these Warm Up activities have great value in helping everyone relax and make the transition from the week's pressures.*

*If your group members are young Christians, chances are that several of the couples
won't know each other well. This first Warm Up will allow them to learn some basic facts
about each other and to verbalize what they hope to learn from the study. If you wish, you
could add another "Getting to Know You" type of question.*

*If the class is too large to allow time for everyone to share (i.e., more than 12), divide into two
or more smaller groups to encourage full participation at the start of the session.*

1. List below the names of the couples in your group, their occupations and the number of years they have been married.

   _____

   _____

   _____

   _____

   *Tip: Ask your mate to share this information about your relationship as a couple. As
   people share, have everyone write down at least one interesting fact about each couple on their handouts.*

2. What is one thing about the Christian life that you would like to learn in this
   study?

   _____

   Tip: Ask everyone to think for a few moments and then ask group members to share their responses. People may respond by saying they'd like to learn to pray more effectively or learn how to study the Bible, etc. If nobody mentions that he or she wants to "learn how to live a genuine Christian life," this will be a good place for you to briefly mention the purposes of this study as outlined in the introduction of this leader's guide.

(25-35 Minutes)

This *Blueprints* section will help couples explore some of the obstacles they may encounter as they seek to grow together in Christ.

I. The No-Growth Dilemma
(10-15 Minutes)

Students are on page 38.

Tip: Choose one of the class members to read the following case study, which illustrates where many people are today in their Christian walk. Then encourage everyone in the group to participate in answering the questions that follow. Be prepared to expand or clarify their answers, if necessary, being cautious about trying to "improve" every answer they give. A pattern of leader additions to all class member comments is very inhibiting to open sharing within a group of adults.

Case Study

Thirty-Eight Years Old, but Still Drinking Milk from a Bottle

Chuck had the sort of credentials a successful doctor dreams about. He achieved the top grades in his high school class, graduated with honors from Harvard and breezed through Harvard Medical School. He decided to specialize in pediatric surgery, and for several years he endured the grueling life of an intern and resident as he learned his specialty.

After completing his residency, Chuck returned home to Chicago and soon had a good practice going. Confident, skilled and well-liked, he seemed to have strong leadership skills. So when Chuck and his wife, Marcie, joined a local church, it seemed natural to their pastor to get them involved in some sort of leadership position.

That's where the troubles began. Marcie did very well teaching a Sunday School class for third graders. But soon after Chuck began teaching a class for young couples, attendance at the class began to fall. "His teaching is just too shallow," one couple said. "He hardly knows the Bible at all."

When the pastor asked Chuck how often he studied the Bible, Chuck replied, "Marcie seems to enjoy that more than I do, and besides, she has the freedom to attend women's Bible studies. I never have the time."

Chuck also was asked to head a committee looking at options for building a new sanctuary. Soon the pastor began hearing reports of contention in the meetings. "Chuck wants to run things his own way," one man said. "He never listens to anyone."

While Chuck's pediatric clinic flourished, he seemed out of his element at church. "You'd never know that he's been a Christian for 20 years," sighed his pastor.

A. What is Chuck's problem?

_____

Answer: Personal and professional growth is no guarantee of spiritual growth. People can make great achievements in their career and even in development of their talents and still make little progress in understanding the Lord's will for their lives. Chuck has apparently never made the effort to grow in his faith the way he has in his professional skills. The mistake some churches make is choosing some people to take leadership positions on the basis of their social maturity or professional abilities rather than their spiritual maturity.

B. Read 1 Corinthians 3:1-3. How do you think a person gets to the point where he or she has been a Christian for many years but is still a spiritual "baby"?

_____

Possible Answer: Sometimes Christians are unwilling to commit every area of their lives to the Lord, and so they remain at an immature level. Sometimes they don't grow because of ignorance, and because they aren't part of a fellowship of believers who are committed to knowing and living God's Word. In either case, they allow the priorities and worries and cares of the world to arrest their spiritual growth.

C. What would happen to Chuck if he devoted the same type of energy to growing spiritually as he gives to growing in his medical skills?

_____

Answer: He would see spiritual growth and development. He would begin to mature as a Christian.

Tip: Read aloud statement D, then invite responses to the questions which follow.

D. Whether it be the rapid development of a newborn child or the first blossoming of a fruit tree, we naturally expect to see growth in all living things. Our life in Christ, too, is meant to be an exciting experience of growth.

   1. Let's say that you love apples and you want to grow your own apple tree. What would you need to do to ensure that this tree grows and bears good fruit?

   _____

Answer: Plant it where it gets the proper amount of sunshine, make sure it gets enough water and fertilizer, etc.

   2. How would you compare this analogy to Christian growth?

   _____

   What do you think a young Christian, or a Christian like Chuck, needs in order to become more mature in his or her faith?

   _____

Answer: A Christian also needs "nutrients" in order to grow. These usually include God's Word, fellowship with other Christians, communion with the Lord, worship and a regular ministry. We'll be looking at these during the remainder of the study.

II. Obstacles to Growth (10-15 Minutes)

Students are on page 39.

Tip: Divide the class into small groups of no more than five or six per group. Briefly share your own response to question C to set a pattern of openness in the group. Then assign the groups to discuss questions A, B and C. Allow five to seven minutes for the groups to interact. As the groups work, mingle among them offering assistance if needed. Then invite volunteers from each group to share their groups' responses to the first two questions.

A. What do you think prevents some Christians from growing spiritually?

_____

Possible Answers: Lack of knowledge. Lack of desire to grow. Some Christians have never had someone come alongside them, challenge them and model the Christian life for them. Sometimes Christians want to grow and know what to do, but they are so preoccupied with other desires or responsibilities that they fail to give spiritual growth the priority it should have in their lives.

B. Read Mark 4:1-9,13-20. According to this passage, what are some things that prevent people from growing spiritually?

_____

Possible Answers: Many people have the wrong "soil" in their hearts. The rocky soil in the parable represents those who, like Chuck in the above case study, don't allow the gospel to become deeply rooted in their lives. When troubles come, they don't have the depth of a relationship with God that they need to withstand the troubles. Many people in America today have "thorny soil" in their hearts. The cares of the world and a delight in material possessions prevents growth.

Tip: If any groups have difficulty with this question, suggest that they look at the four types of soil one at a time.

C. Have you ever gone through a period in your life where you didn't grow in your faith? If you can, tell about what characterized your life at that time. Why didn't you grow?

_____

Tip: Ask for a show of hands of those who recalled a time in their lives when they did not grow as a Christian. Invite volunteers to share any factors in that lack of growth which have not already been mentioned to the class. Then ask for volunteers to respond to question D.

D. Why would you say that so many Christian couples don't experience growth together?

_____

Possible Answer: The biggest problem many couples face is that they don't make growing together in Christ a priority. You need to carve time out of your schedule to pray and study the Bible together and to discuss what you're learning about the Lord. Many couples know they need to spend this time together, but they fail to act decisively and commit to a certain time. Other couples face an additional problem because one individual is making the effort to grow spiritually while the other is not.

III. Evidences of Growth
(5 Minutes)

Students are on page 39.

Tip: Instruct each person to spend a few moments answering the questions individually. Then either you or your mate share your response to the questions. Next, invite volunteers to share their answers with the class. In sharing responses to question B, remind the class of the first ground rule for the series: "Share nothing about your marriage which will embarrass your mate."

A. Read 2 Corinthians 5:17. What are some ways you've become a "new creature" since you became a Christian?

_____

How has your life changed?

_____

B. How have you seen your mate's life change since he or she became a Christian?

_____

(5 Minutes)

Students are on page 40.

Each *HomeBuilders Project* builds upon what you've learned during the *Blueprints* section and is essential for couples to complete together before the next meeting. This first project is designed to help couples evaluate their spiritual growth.

Make a date with your mate to meet in the next few days to complete *HomeBuilders Project #1*. This will aid you as a couple in the process of growing together in Christ. Your leader will ask you at the next session to share one thing from this experience.

_____   _____   _____
Date   Time   Location

Tip: Distribute copies of the Make a Date handout. Instruct couples to take a few moments and set a time this week when they will complete HomeBuilders Project #1 together. Encourage them to set aside 20 to 30 minutes in which to respond to the items individually and discuss their answers together.

Emphasize that this is not homework to earn a passing grade, but a highly significant time of interaction that will improve communication and understanding.

Point out that the projects are written to lead couples to definite application and action. In some cases, participants may have to face some uncomfortable issues as they look at making changes in their attitudes, lifestyles and schedules. Sometimes the questions may bring up some sensitive issues. The intention is not to start arguments but to stimulate honest reflection and interaction. While not every question will affect every couple in the same way, the time spent thinking and talking will be more than worthwhile for any couple.

Tell the group that at the next session you will ask each couple to share one thing they discovered or discussed during the HomeBuilders Project. Also, urge group members to bring their calendars to the next session as an aid in scheduling their next date with their mates. The books listed at the end of each session are not required, but are recommended to reinforce and expand the concepts dealt with in the group session. Encourage couples to locate one or all of these books and read from them before the next session. One effective idea is for one spouse to read aloud to the other, either in the morning before going to work or in the evening before retiring.

How to Be Sure You Are a Christian, by Bill Bright.

This booklet in the Transferable Concepts series briefly, yet effectively, presents the practical steps for gaining assurance of salvation.

My Utmost for His Highest, by Oswald Chambers.

This devotional classic offers encouragement to face life's challenges every day.

Authentic Christianity, by Ray Stedman.

This fresh study on the sharp distinctions between the phony and the genuine expressions of the Christian life is based on the text of 2 Corinthians 2:14—6:13.

Dismiss in prayer, then invite everyone to enjoy a time of fellowship and refreshments. Informal opportunities to build relationships are a key ingredient in the success of this series. If necessary, shorten the study time in this session so that people do not feel pressured to leave quickly.

SESSION 1

Obstacles to Growth as a Couple

Focus

All couples face barriers to growth in their Christian lives.

Warm-Up

1. List below the names of couples in your group, their occupations and the number of years they have been married.

   _____

   _____

   _____

   _____

2. What is one thing about the Christian life that you would like to learn in this study?

   _____

I. The No-Growth Dilemma
Case Study

Thirty-Eight Years Old, but Still Drinking Milk from a Bottle

Chuck had the sort of credentials a successful doctor dreams about. He achieved the top grades in his high school class, graduated with honors from Harvard and breezed through Harvard Medical School. He decided to specialize in pediatric surgery, and for several years he endured the grueling life of an intern and resident as he learned his specialty.

After completing his residency, Chuck returned home to Chicago and soon had a good practice going. Confident, skilled and well-liked, he seemed to have strong leadership skills. So when Chuck and his wife, Marcie, joined a local church, it seemed natural to their pastor to get them involved in some sort of leadership position.

That's where the troubles began. Marcie did very well teaching a Sunday School class for third graders. But soon after Chuck began teaching a class for young couples, attendance at the class began to fall. "His teaching is just too shallow," one couple said. "He hardly knows the Bible at all."

When the pastor asked Chuck how often he studied the Bible, Chuck replied, "Marcie seems to enjoy that more than I do, and besides, she has the freedom to attend women's Bible studies. I never have the time."

Chuck also was asked to head a committee looking at options for building a new sanctuary. Soon the pastor began hearing reports of contention in the meetings. "Chuck wants to run things his own way," one man said. "He never listens to anyone."

While Chuck's pediatric clinic flourished, he seemed out of his element at church. "You'd never know that he's been a Christian for 20 years," sighed his pastor.

A. What is Chuck's problem?

_____

B. Read 1 Corinthians 3:1-3. How do you think a person gets to the point where he or she has been a Christian for many years but is still a spiritual "baby"?

_____

C. What would happen to Chuck if he devoted the same type of energy to growing spiritually as he gives to growing in his medical skills?

_____

D. Whether it be the rapid development of a newborn child or the first blossoming of a fruit tree, we naturally expect to see growth in all living things. Our life in Christ, too, is meant to be an exciting experience of growth.

1. Let's say that you love apples and you want to grow your own apple tree. What would you need to do to ensure that this tree grows and bears good fruit?

_____

2. How would you compare this analogy to Christian growth?

_____

What do you think a young Christian, or a Christian like Chuck, needs in order to become more mature in his or her faith?

_____

II. Obstacles to Growth

A. What do you think prevents some Christians from growing spiritually?

_____

B. Read Mark 4:1-9,13-20. According to this passage, what are some things that prevent people from growing spiritually?

_____

C. Have you ever gone through a period in your life where you didn't grow in your faith? If you can, tell about what characterized your life at that time. Why didn't you grow?

_____

D. Why would you say that so many Christian couples don't experience growth together?

_____

III. Evidences of Growth

A. Read 2 Corinthians 5:17. What are some ways you've become a "new creature" since you became a Christian?

_____

How has your life changed?

_____

B. How have you seen your mate's life change since he or she became a Christian?

_____

Each **HomeBuilders Project** builds upon what you've learned during the **Blueprints** section and is essential for couples to complete together before the next meeting. This first project is designed to help couples evaluate their spiritual growth.

Make a date with your mate to meet in the next few days to complete **HomeBuilders Project #1**. This will aid you as a couple in the process of growing together in Christ. Your leader will ask you at the next session to share one thing from this experience.

_____   _____   _____
Date   Time   Location

How to Be Sure You Are a Christian, by Bill Bright.
This booklet in the Transferable Concepts series briefly yet effectively presents the practical steps for gaining assurance of salvation.

My Utmost for His Highest, by Oswald Chambers.
This devotional classic offers encouragement to face life's challenges every day.

Authentic Christianity, by Ray Stedman.
This fresh study on the sharp distinctions between the phony and the genuine expressions of the Christian life is based on the text of 2 Corinthians 2:14—6:13.

Individually: 10-15 Minutes

1. Draw a line that traces your spiritual growth pattern since you became a Christian. Have your line go up during times of spiritual growth, flat during times of spiritual stagnation and down during times of falling away from God.

What factors have caused the various phases in your spiritual growth?

2. Now draw a similar chart illustrating how you perceive your mate's spiritual growth:

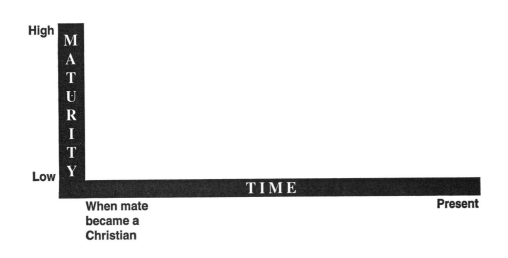

Interact as a Couple: 10-15 Minutes

1. Review the group session briefly and share what points were especially meaningful to you.

2. Take a look at the spiritual growth charts you filled out and explain your reasoning to each other.

3. Some couples have a problem in their marriage because they are growing in the Christian life at dramatically different rates; one partner is experiencing dynamic growth while the other is inching along. Do you think this is true in your marriage? Why or why not?

    _____

    If it is, what can you do about it?

    _____

4. Conclude your time together by reading the following personal pledge statement:

    "I pledge to you that I will use the next 11 sessions of this HomeBuilders study to build, strengthen and encourage our marriage. I will make this study a priority in my schedule by faithfully keeping our dates, working through the projects and participating in the group discussions. You have my word on it."

    _____   _____

    (signed)   (date)

    Will you honor your mate by making this pledge your special commitment to him or her for the coming weeks? If so, sign your name in the space provided on your mate's project page to document your commitment.

5. Pray together, asking the Lord to guide you to achieve new levels of spiritual growth in your marriage.

Remember to bring your calendar to the next session so you can **Make a Date.**

SESSION 2

Essentials for Growth as a Couple

OBJECTIVES

You will help your group members start building a foundation for Christian growth as you guide them to:

- Share how their lives have changed since they've become Christians;
- Learn three essentials for spiritual growth; and
- Realize the importance of growing together as a couple.

COMMENTS

Session One focused on the barriers that individuals and couples face in growing as Christians. Growing together in Christ is the theme and focus of our study here in Session Two. The first essential for such growth is new life in Christ. Be sensitive to those individuals or couples who struggle with accepting God's purposes as their own. Your warmth and acceptance can have a significant role in someone being willing to really put the principles of these sessions into practice.

STARTING THE SESSION

1. Be sure you duplicate copies of the Session Two reproducible handouts for each individual. Also have Bibles and extra pens or pencils available.

2. Welcome group members individually as they arrive. Introduce those who do not know each other and assist them in beginning some informal conversation. Name tags will help couples connect names with faces. Beverages and a light refreshment will help people begin to enjoy this time together.

3. Start the session on time, even if everyone is not yet present. Briefly share a few positive feelings about leading this study:

The Christian life is one of exciting growth as you establish a solid relationship with Christ.

Students are on page 50.

(10-15 Minutes)

The Warm Up is intended to set a friendly, enjoyable tone from the beginning of each session. Once your group becomes well-acquainted, these Warm Up activities still have great value in helping everyone feel good about making the effort to attend as well as building a comfort level that contributes to the willingness to be open in sharing during the session. The Warm Up time also establishes the climate of accountability as people share insights gained from the HomeBuilders Project.

Tip: Ask for a show of hands of those who found it difficult to keep the commitment to meet together and complete the first HomeBuilders Project. Affirm those who did complete the project. Ask everyone to stand, walk around and ask at least three other class members to share their responses to the following three questions on their handouts. Share your own responses first to continue setting an example of open sharing.

1. What is one thing you and your mate did together this past week—that you can tell about?

   _____

2. What is one thing about the *HomeBuilders Project* that you enjoyed?

   _____

3. What is one insight you gained from the *HomeBuilders Project*?

   _____

   Tip: After three to four minutes of interaction, invite everyone to return to their seats. Ask volunteers to tell some of the things they heard that couples did together during the past week. Then ask for others to share the most interesting answer they heard as to what someone enjoyed about the project. After several people respond, ask for people who have not had a chance to share yet to tell about insights they heard that people gained.

(25-35 Minutes)

This session's *Blueprints section is designed to help couples discover three essentials for spiritual growth. First, couples will explore the teaching of John 15:1-8 about a key to spiritual growth: being in the vine and bearing fruit. Along with the biblical study of John 15, we'll look at two important attitudes that foster growth together in Christ.*

I. New Life in Christ *(10-15 Minutes)*

Students are on page 51.

A. Share with the class some of the ways you feel you have grown since becoming a Christian.

_____

Tip: Share one or two ways that being a Christian has changed your life.

B. Read John 15:1-8. According to this passage, what is the key to spiritual growth?

_____

Answer: Abiding in Christ.

Tip: Introduce John 15, telling the class that these are words Jesus spoke to His closest followers shortly before His execution. Then read aloud John 15:1-8, asking class members to listen for the answer to question B.

C. What does it mean to "abide in" Christ?

_____

Answer: When you asked Christ to come into your heart, He began living (abiding) in you. But you cannot grow unless you, in turn, abide in Him by seeking to know Him and drawing upon His strength. Christ is the vine; you are a branch. As a branch, you are connected to Christ, and you draw your life from Him. We'll talk about ways to do that in future sessions.

Lead the class in reading aloud the first HomeBuilders Principle:

HOMEBUILDERS PRINCIPLE #1:
The true Christian life is an exciting, everyday relationship with the living Christ.

Students are on page 51.

II. A Teachable Heart
(5-10 Minutes)

Comment: The first essential for a growing Christian life is maintaining a vital relationship with Christ. The second essential has to do with our inner attitude.

Tip: Divide the class in half. Ask everyone to find one or two partners. Pause for a moment to be sure no one is left out and that all small groups have a Bible. Then assign the groups in one half of the class to complete question A, while the other half works to complete question B.

A person with a teachable heart has two qualities:

A. First, he or she is able to hear. Read Hebrews 5:11,12. **What do you think it means to be "dull of hearing"?**

_____

Possible Answers: Unmotivated, passive, disinterested, distracted, not seeing the importance of what you are listening to.

B. Second, a person with a teachable heart is committed to doing what he or she has learned. Read James 1:22. **Why do you think it's so important to do what you are commanded in Scripture?**

_____

Possible Answers: If you don't act upon God's Word and do what He says, you cut off fellowship from Him. What often sets apart a growing Christian from one who is stuck is that the growing Christian is applying the Word to his or her life and acting upon it rather than merely listening to it.

III. A Commitment to Encourage Each Other (10 Minutes)

Students are on page 51.

A. If both you and your mate continue to grow in your relationships with Christ, how will your growth affect your marriage?

_____

Answer: As you mature in Christ you will mature in your love for each other.

B. What will happen in your marriage if one of you is growing spiritually, but the other is not?

_____

Possible Answers: There will be a loss of fellowship. There will be a certain frustration and difficulty communicating with one another.

C. How do you think you could avoid such a situation?

_____

Possible Answers: Make sure you are both growing in Christ. Encourage each other to draw on the resources of your new life in Christ. As already stated, carve time out of your schedule to spend time together praying and studying God's Word.

Tip: Lead the class in reading aloud HomeBuilders Principle #2, then ask for volunteers to suggest responses to question D. This is an open-ended question. You as a leader should think of some ways that you and your mate have encouraged each other; your answers may help others think of what they've done.

HOMEBUILDERS PRINCIPLE #2:

As two people grow closer to God, they will experience greater oneness in their marriage.

D. You are an important part of encouraging your mate to grow spiritually. What are some ways you can encourage your mate in this area?

_____

Possible Answers: *Some people have problems finding time in their schedules to spend with the Lord. Look for ways to help your mate find this time. For example, you might volunteer to help with some household responsibility that is normally not yours. If television steals too many of your evening hours, agree to turn the set off and spend time with the Lord instead. Your encouragement also may be verbal: pointing your mate to the Lord or to a specific Scripture in times of trouble, gently helping your mate stop self-criticism, etc. Perhaps most important is demonstrating complete acceptance and unconditional love for your mate. This type of love is only possible through the power of Christ, and seeing that love in you will point your mate to the Lord.*

Students are on page 52.

(5 Minutes)

Comment: *"Each HomeBuilders Project builds upon what you've learned during the session and is essential for you to complete together before the next meeting. This session's project is designed to help you choose some specific steps you can take to encourage your mates."*

Ask each couple to look at the *Make a Date* section and to agree on a time this week to complete HomeBuilders Project #2 together. Persuade couples to set aside 20-30 minutes for the project. Emphasize again that this is not homework to earn a passing grade, but a highly significant time of interaction that will improve communication and understanding.

Tell the group that at the next session you will again ask each couple to share one thing they discovered or discussed during the HomeBuilders Project. Also, urge group members to bring their calendars to each session as an aid in scheduling their next date with their mates.

Make a date with your mate to meet in the next few days to complete *HomeBuilders Project #2*. This will aid you as a couple in continuing the process of growing together in Christ. Your leader will ask you at the next session to share one thing from this experience.

Date	Time	Location

Recommended Reading

The books listed at the end of each session are not required, but are recommended to reinforce and expand the concepts dealt with in the group session. Encourage couples to locate one or all of these books and read from them before the next session. One effective idea is for one spouse to read aloud to the other, either in the morning before going to work or in the evening before retiring.

How to Walk in the Spirit, by Bill Bright.

This booklet is another in the Transferable Concepts series, briefly yet effectively presenting practical steps for becoming a growing Christian.

The Imitation of Christ, by Thomas á Kempis.

As the most widely read Christian devotional in the world for 500 years, this book is certain to enhance the growth of all Christians.

Abiding in Christ, by James E. Rosscup.

This entire book is devoted to the study of John 15, discussing the vital issues of abiding in Christ.

Dismiss in prayer or invite group members to volunteer one-sentence prayers focused on the essentials for growth in Christ. Then invite everyone to enjoy a time of fellowship and refreshments.

Essentials for Growth as a Couple

The Christian life is one of exciting growth as you establish a solid relationship with Christ.

1. What is one thing you and your mate did together this past week—that you can tell about?

   _____

2. What is one thing about the **HomeBuilders Project** that you enjoyed?

   _____

3. What is one insight you gained from the **HomeBuilders Project**?

   _____

I. New Life in Christ

A. Share with the class some of the ways you feel you have grown since becoming a Christian.

_____

B. Read John 15:1-8. According to this passage, what is the key to spiritual growth?

_____

C. What does it mean to "abide in" Christ?

_____

HOMEBUILDERS PRINCIPLE #1:

The true Christian life is an exciting, everyday relationship with the living Christ.

II. A Teachable Heart

A person with a teachable heart has two qualities:

A. First, he or she is able to hear. Read Hebrews 5:11,12. What do you think it means to be "dull of hearing"?

_____

B. Second, a person with a teachable heart is committed to doing what he or she has learned. Read James 1:22. Why do you think it's so important to do what you are commanded in Scripture?

_____

III. A Commitment to Encourage Each Other

A. If both you and your mate continue to grow in your relationships with Christ, how will your growth affect your marriage?

_____

B. What will happen in your marriage if one of you is growing spiritually, but the other is not?

_____

C. How do you think you could avoid such a situation?

_____

HOMEBUILDERS PRINCIPLE #2:

As two people grow closer to God, they will experience greater oneness in their marriage.

D. You are an important part of encouraging your mate to grow spiritually. What are some ways you can encourage your mate in this area?

_____

Make a date with your mate to meet in the next few days to complete **HomeBuilders Project #2**. This will aid you as a couple in continuing the process of growing together in Christ. Your leader will ask you at the next session to share one thing from this experience.

_____   _____   _____

Date   Time   Location

How to Walk in the Spirit, by Bill Bright.

This booklet is another in the Transferable Concepts series, briefly yet effectively presenting practical steps for becoming a growing Christian.

The Imitation of Christ, by Thomas á Kempis.

As the most widely read Christian devotional in the world for 500 years, this book is certain to enhance the growth of all Christians.

Abiding in Christ, by James E. Rosscup.

This entire book is devoted to the study of John 15, discussing the vital issues of abiding in Christ.

Individually: 10 Minutes

1. What are three things you can begin doing to help your mate grow spiritually?

   _____

2. What should you *stop* doing in order to help your mate grow?

   _____

3. What can your mate do to help you grow spiritually?

   _____

4. What would you like your mate to stop doing?

   _____

Interact as a Couple: 10-20 Minutes

1. Review the group session briefly and share what points were especially meaningful to you.
2. Share the answers each of you wrote for the questions in the individual section.
3. Conclude your time together by praying, asking the Lord to guide you to achieve new levels of spiritual growth in your marriage.

Remember to bring your calendar to the next session so you can **Make a Date**.

The Benefits of Prayer in Marriage

OBJECTIVES

You will help your group members discover the importance of prayer in spiritual growth as you guide them to:

- Think of reasons why Christians don't pray more than they do; and
- Discover what the Bible says about the benefits of prayer.

COMMENTS

Duplicate enough Session Three handouts so that each class member has a personal copy.

Prayer promotes growth both in your relationship with God and in your relationship with your mate.

Students are on page 61.

(15-20 Minutes)

The Warm Up will help your group members begin to talk about prayer and will help them evaluate the perceptions about prayer that they developed while growing up. In addition, the first question is important because it gives participants the opportunity to tell others what they learned during their HomeBuilders Project, and it gives you the opportunity to hold them accountable for getting the HomeBuilders Projects done.

Greet people warmly as they arrive. Engage them in informal conversation about events of the week until it is time to begin.

Start the session on time, even if everyone is not yet present.

Ask for a show of hands of the couples who kept their date with each other and completed HomeBuilders Project #2. Share one thing you learned as you and your mate completed the project, then ask for volunteers to share something they learned. Affirm those who share as well as any others who also completed the project.

1. Begin this session by sharing one thing you learned from *HomeBuilders Project #2.*

   _____

   Tip: Divide the class into groups of no more than five of six per group. Starting with the person in each group who most recently completed (or even attempted) a household repair (of any kind), have each person share their answers to questions 2a and b. Be prepared to share something from your own childhood to get the group started answering these questions.

2. Whether or not you grew up in a Christian home, you learned something about prayer as you grew up and observed the attitudes and practices of family, friends, church members or even characters in television shows and movies.

   a. What kinds of prayers do you recall praying as a child?

   _____

   Possible Answers: For many as they were growing up, prayer was just something done at dinnertime and before bed. Their prayers were rote recitations that they used day after day.

   b. What do you think you learned about prayer when you were a child?

   _____

   What attitudes and habits did you pick up?

   _____

Possible Answers: Some people may realize that their prayers today are very similar to the ones they prayed as a child. Others may have grown up in homes where nobody prayed, and so they learned that prayer is not important.

If time permits invite volunteers to share with the class any answers they found interesting.

(25-35 Minutes)

The following Blueprints section highlights some common barriers and major benefits to prayer, and then it outlines some of the major components of prayer.

I. The Barriers to Prayer
   (5-10 Minutes)

Students are on page 62.

Tip: Since the Warm Up may have already touched on some of the negative things people in the group learned about prayer, you may not want to spend too much time here. However, it's important to touch on the barriers to prayer, so that your group members can identify what keeps them from praying more. Invite volunteers to respond to the following questions.

   A. **What do you think the average Christian thinks about prayer?**

   _____

   What keeps people from praying more than they do?

   _____

Possible Answers: Christians often have bad attitudes about prayer, and these attitudes keep them from praying more. They think prayer is boring, difficult, repetitive, ineffective. Some Christians wonder if prayer is really necessary; if God already knows everything, why pray? Or they may wonder why God doesn't seem to answer their prayers more often. Another reason Christians may not pray is that they don't know how to do it or simply feel uncomfortable when trying to pray.

   B. **Why do you think many Christian couples fail to spend much time together in prayer?**

   _____

Possible Answers: Christian couples often know they should pray together, but they just don't do it. They haven't made prayer together a regular habit, and they let other activities and priorities take precedence. Again, they may not pray because they don't feel comfortable doing it.

C. How do you think most men feel about praying with their wives?

_____

How do wives feel about praying with their husbands?

_____

Possible Answers: Men often feel awkward, inadequate, unsure of themselves. Men often like to be in charge, but prayer is not an activity in which they feel confident. Also, prayer may make them feel more vulnerable than they want to feel. Many men grew up in homes where religion was considered "women's turf." Most wives love to pray with their husbands and may feel frustrated when their husbands don't take the lead in doing so.

II. The Benefits of Prayer (10 Minutes)

Students are on page 62.

Tip: This is probably the most important section of this session. If your group members can grasp the fact that prayer doesn't have to be lifeless, that they can grow spiritually and experience God's peace, they will be motivated to pray more. Assign each of the four verses below to one quarter of the class. Ask everyone to silently read their assigned verse and think of their answer to question A. After allowing time for people to locate and read their verse, ask for volunteers from each section to share their answers.

A. What do the following verses tell you about how prayer will help you grow in your relationship with God?

   1. John 16:24

   _____

Answer: This verse invites us to ask our Father in heaven for whatever we need. It's really like a blank check: "Ask, and you will receive." Prayer also helps us grow in our relationship with God by giving us joy.

   2. James 1:5

   _____

Answer: If you lack wisdom, this verse encourages you to ask God to give it to you. This is the type of wisdom that will greatly enrich your life and help you with both the major and minor decisions you must make.

3. James 4:8

_____

Answer: This verse shows the reciprocal nature of prayer: "Draw near to God and He will draw near to you." Prayer is not simply reaching out into the dark or speaking into the unknown. As you reach out to God in prayer, you will feel His presence, His closeness. There's nothing more exciting than to experience God in this way.

4. Philippians 4:6,7

_____

Answer: Prayer is the vehicle for delivering us from our anxieties. The Lord invites us to bring everything to Him in prayer and not to worry about anything. As a result of giving all our requests to Him, we receive the peace of God. And with the peace of God in our lives, we are going to mature spiritually.

Tip: The next question is important because it allows people to see that the verses they've read are really true. You or your spouse should be prepared to share one or two experiences from your own life, then invite volunteers to share any similar experiences. To keep from intimidating people, avoid sharing any highly dramatic incidents that might make others feel like their experiences are "small potatoes" by comparison.

B. Share about a time when you experienced the truths of the previous verses. How have you received God's wisdom or peace or experienced Him through prayer?

_____

Tip: After several people share, read aloud 1 John 5:14,15 and invite responses to question C.

C. Read 1 John 5:14,15. Why do you think God wants us to ask Him to answer specific requests?

_____

Answer: It's a confidence builder. Specific answers to specific requests build our appreciation and level of confidence in God's great power and love in our lives.

Tip: Be prepared to give an illustration of your own in response to question D, then invite volunteers to share from their experiences.

D. Share how you've seen God answer a specific prayer request.

Make a Date

Students are on page 63.

(5 Minutes)

Each HomeBuilders Project is absolutely essential for couples to do together during the week. This week, couples will focus on how they can pray together.

Ask each couple to look at the Make a Date section of the handout, and then agree on a time this week to complete HomeBuilders Project #3 together. Encourage couples to set aside 20-30 minutes to respond to the items individually and then discuss their answers.

Make a date with your mate to meet in the next few days to complete *HomeBuilders Project #3.* This project will help you as a couple in developing a more consistent prayer life.

Date	Time	Location

Recommended Reading

Again, the reading is not required, but is highly recommended to reinforce and expand the concepts dealt with in the group session. Encourage couples to locate one or all of these books and spend some time with them before the next session.

How to Pray, by Bill Bright.

This concise and confidence-building booklet will point you toward a more meaningful prayer life.

Power Through Prayer, by E. M. Bounds.

This is possibly the most widely read pamphlet on prayer, and it will be a great encouragement for improving your prayer life.

Remind the group that at the next session you will ask each couple to share one thing they discovered or discussed during their HomeBuilders Project.

Also, remind the group members to bring their calendars to the next session as an aid in scheduling their next date with their mates.

Dismiss in prayer or invite class members to volunteer one-sentence prayers encouraging one another to grow in their prayer lives. Then invite everyone to enjoy a time of fellowship and refreshments.

SESSION 3

The Benefits of Prayer in Marriage

Focus

Prayer promotes growth both in your relationship with God and in your relationship with your mate.

Warm-Up

1. Begin this session by sharing one thing you learned from **HomeBuilders Project #2**.

_____

2. Whether or not you grew up in a Christian home, you learned something about prayer as you grew up and observed the attitudes and practices of family, friends, church members or even characters in television shows and movies.

   a. What kinds of prayers do you recall praying as a child?

   _____

   b. What do you think you learned about prayer when you were a child?

   _____

   What attitudes and habits did you pick up?

   _____

I. The Barriers to Prayer

A. What do you think the average Christian thinks about prayer?

_____

What keeps people from praying more than they do?

_____

B. Why do you think many Christian couples fail to spend much time together in prayer?

_____

C. How do you think most men feel about praying with their wives?

_____

How do wives feel about praying with their husbands?

_____

II. The Benefits of Prayer

A. What do the following verses tell you about how prayer will help you grow in your relationship with God?

   1. John 16:24

   _____

   2. James 1:5

   _____

   3. James 4:8

   _____

   4. Philippians 4:6,7

   _____

B. Share about a time when you experienced the truths of the previous verses. How have you received God's wisdom or peace or experienced Him through prayer?

_____

C. Read 1 John 5:14,15. Why do you think God wants us to ask Him to answer specific requests?

_____

D. Share how you've seen God answer a specific prayer request.

_____

Make a date with your mate to meet in the next few days to complete **HomeBuilders Project #3.** This project will help you as a couple in developing a more consistent prayer life.

_____   _____   _____
        Date   Time   Location

How to Pray, by Bill Bright.

This concise and confidence-building booklet will point you toward a more meaningful prayer life.

Power through Prayer, by E. M. Bounds.

This is possibly the most widely read pamphlet on prayer, and it will be a great encouragement for improving your prayer life.

Individually: 10-15 Minutes

1. Identify the two or three things that make prayer difficult for you as an individual.

   _____

2. Identify the two or three things that make prayer difficult for you as a couple.

   _____

Interact as a Couple: 10-15 Minutes

1. Share with each other the insights you gained from your individual time.
2. How do you think your marriage would benefit if you were to pray together regularly as a couple?

   _____

3. What steps can you take to resolve one of these difficulties?

   _____

Remember to bring your calendar for **Make a Date** to the next session.

SESSION 4

The Power of Prayer in Marriage

OBJECTIVES

You will help your group members discover the importance of prayer in spiritual growth as you guide them to:

- Reflect on the value of prayer in marriage;
- Identify how regular prayer together can change their marriage relationship; and
- Learn three components of prayer.

COMMENTS

Duplicate enough Session Four handouts so that each class member has a personal copy.

Effective prayer includes praise, confession and supplication.

Students are on page 73.

(15-20 Minutes)

The Warm Up will help your group members continue to talk about prayer, and it gives you the opportunity to hold them accountable for getting the HomeBuilders Projects done.

    Greet people warmly as they arrive. Give each group member a 3x5-inch index card. Ask each one to write a statement about prayer—what prayer means to him or her, how it affects him or her, etc.—on his or her card. One example might be "Prayer changes people rather than things." When they have completed their statements, have them return their cards to you.

    Start the session on time, even if everyone is not yet present.

    Tip: *Ask for a show of hands of the couples who kept their date with each other and completed last session's HomeBuilders Project. Affirm those who did so and invite volunteers to tell one insight they gained from last session's project.*

Begin this session by sharing one thing you learned from HomeBuilders Project #3.

Tip: *After several people have shared about their HomeBuilders Project, redistribute the index cards insuring that they don't get their own cards. Have each person read the card that you have given them. Ask them if they agree or disagree with the statement they have read and have them explain why.*

(30-40 Minutes)

Students are on page 74.

I. The Power of Prayer in Marriage
(20-25 Minutes)

    Tip: *Ask each person to silently read the introductory sentences on this section of their handouts. Then ask volunteers to tell their answers to questions A, B and C. Seek to involve as many people as possible, encouraging them to be as specific as* *possible in their answers. Invite people to share examples from their own experience which illustrate their answers. Be prepared to ask follow-up questions if necessary to stimulate people to think and participate. A few sample questions are provided below.*

This Blueprints section is designed to help couples discover the power of prayer in marriage. People often think of the power of prayer in terms of church or their individual lives but not so much in terms of marriage.

Most of us long for closeness and companionship in our marriages. We may try to fulfill the longing through activities and projects like fixing up the house or taking a trip together; yet when the projects are complete, we often still feel a void.

A. What would happen in a marriage relationship if one partner was not confessing sin to God?

_____

Answer: It would hurt the relationship. The person harboring unconfessed sin would be unable to grow in his or her walk with God, and this would create a barrier between the two marriage partners. This barrier would be greatest if the unconfessed sin had been committed against the mate.

Ask: "How could one of us respond when we sense that our mate is holding on to unconfessed sin? How can we encourage each other to be open and specific in our prayers of confession?"

B. How do you think any tendencies toward self-centeredness in your marriage would be affected if you regularly praised God together?

_____

Answer: Self-centeredness would be diminished. We would be refocused on the greatness of God in our lives, rather than our own needs, desires and limitations.

Ask: "How can one person in a marriage encourage his or her mate to praise God more?"

C. How do you think praying together would affect your growth and unity as a couple?

_____

Answer: It would accelerate growth and encourage unity. Praying together is an important part of building a great marriage.

Ask: "How can praying together affect your love for each other? Your communication with each other? Your respect for one another? In what specific areas of your marriage have any of you seen growth as a result of praying together?"

Tip: Read aloud HomeBuilders Principle #3:

HOMEBUILDERS PRINCIPLE #3:

Praying to God together helps produce the cleansing, forgiveness, humility and unity essential to continued growth in marriage.

Tip: Tell how you pray with your mate. Share a few specific examples of times you prayed together and any ways you have found that help make your prayer times meaningful. Then ask everyone to privately answer question D. After a few minutes, invite volunteers to share ideas for making prayer time exciting.

D. Do you pray together often as a couple? If so, how do you do it?

_____

How do you fit it into your schedule?

_____

What can you do to make prayer exciting?

_____

Possible Answers: An approach to prayer that you may want to share as a way to keep prayer times lively is that of "conversational" prayer. This method encourages people to think of prayer as a dialog with God, rather than a monologue in which one person addresses a lengthy speech to God. Guidelines for conversational prayer include:

- *Each person prays about only one thing at a time, then allows the other person to respond;*
- *No new topic is introduced until both persons have commented about the first topic;*
- *Conversational language is used, avoiding religious jargon.*

Students are on page 74.

II. Basic Components of Prayer (10-15 Minutes)

Tip: Call attention to the introductory comments about the basic components of prayer.

Because prayer is talking with God, it's a wonderful way to develop your relationship with Him. However, many people know little about what to do as they pray.

The Psalms of the Bible are among the best-known and best-loved writings of all literature. Many psalms are actually prayers, and from them we can learn about some basic components of prayer.

Tip: Have the class form groups of two or three members. Have everyone turn to Psalm 96. Assign each of the first ten verses to a different pair or trio to read aloud as an expression of praise. Allow a few moments for people to silently read their assigned verses, thinking of the meaning and prayerfully making those thoughts their own. Have the class read the psalm aloud, then invite responses to questions 1 and 2. Be prepared to share your own insights about the benefits of praising God.

A. *Praise:* Psalm 96 illustrates one major component of prayer—praise of God. Praising God means focusing on His character and His deeds and giving Him public acclaim. Read verses 1-10.

1. If you were to spend time consistently praising God, how would that practice affect the way you look at various problems you encounter in life?

_____

Possible Answer: Worship and praise raise our awareness of God's presence in our lives. The more we praise Him, the more we notice the ways He touches every aspect of our experience. Praising God also helps us see that our problems are more insignificant than we feel they are, that He will use even the worst problems to conform us to His image and that He is more powerful than our problems. Also, praising God for a specific quality you appreciate in your mate can be a powerful way to enrich a marriage. It is very hard to have an argument with someone for whom you have been praising God.

Tip: Also share ways you have found to praise Him in the midst of your daily routines.

2. What is something you can praise God for right now?

_____

Tip: Read aloud Psalm 51:1-13, asking class members to follow along, thinking of their answers to questions 1 and 2.

B. *Confession*: Psalm 51 is treasured as one of the greatest expressions of confession. Read verses 1-13, in which King David confesses His transgressions—committing adultery with Bathsheba and sending her husband off to be killed in battle.

1. How would you describe the burden David felt because of his sin?

_____

Answer: David felt defiled and guilty. He lost his joy in the Lord, and he felt dirty for what happened to him. He felt as if he were going to lose the very presence of God in his life.

2. What did David's confession accomplish?

_____

Answer: David asked for forgiveness and cleansing, and we can assume that he received it from the Lord. He was given a renewed perspective on life, his responsibility to God and the work of God in the world. Point out that most people view confession as a prelude to punishment. This is true in most areas of human experience. God's response is totally different.

Tip: Instruct everyone to read 1 John 1:9 silently. Call on a class member to tell what the verse says is the result of confession.

3. Read 1 John 1:9. What happens when you confess a specific sin?

_____

Answer: He is faithful, He keeps His promises, He is just. Since Christ has already paid the penalty for our sins, God would be unjust not to forgive and cleanse His children who confess their sins to Him.

Tip: Encourage each person to take a few moments to ask God to reveal any sin in his or her heart. Then allow a few minutes of silence in which class members can express their confession to God and receive their forgiveness.

Tip: Before getting into Psalm 34 or Matthew 7, ask for a volunteer to define or describe the word "supplication" (an earnest and humble request). Prior to reading the verses, ask the group to think in terms of motivation for prayers that are listed here.

C. *Supplication:* Psalm 34 is often read and quoted to encourage us to bring our needs and desires to God in prayer. This is called supplication. Read verses 4-18.

1. What do you find in these verses that would motivate you to pray regularly?

_____

Answer: This psalm not only talks about what God will do to answer our prayers, but it also discusses what He does in our hearts when we pray.

2. What does Matthew 7:7-11 have to say about making requests to the Lord?

_____

Answer: This passage indicates God's desire for us to make requests to Him. It also shows His desire to "give good gifts" to His children. We shouldn't assume from this verse, however, that God will grant any request we make of Him. First John 5:14 shows that we need to ask "according to His will."

(5 Minutes)

Students are on page 75.

Each HomeBuilders Project is absolutely essential for couples to do together during the week. This week, couples will focus on what they can pray for together.

Ask each couple to look at the Make a Date section of the handout, then agree on a time this week to complete HomeBuilders Project #4 together. Point out that couples will be starting a prayer journal as part of the HomeBuilders Project. Encourage couples to set aside 20-30 minutes to respond to the items individually and then discuss their answers.

Make a date with your mate to meet in the next few days to complete *HomeBuilders Project #4.* This project will help you as a couple to develop a more consistent prayer life.

You'll need to bring a notebook and paper with you when you meet with your mate to complete the *HomeBuilders Project.* Your leader will ask you at the next session to share one experience or insight from your time together.

_____ _____	_____
Date Time	Location

Recommended Reading

Again, the reading is not required, but is highly recommended to reinforce and expand the concepts dealt with in the group session. Encourage couples to locate one or all of these books and spend some time reading them before the next session.

Too Busy Not to Pray, by Bill Hybels.

Most of us have trouble finding time to pray. This book presents a plan for slowing down to be with God.

The Knowledge of the Holy, by A. W. Tozer.

Nothing will have a greater impact on your prayer life than getting to know the One to whom you are praying. This book is a classic guide to that knowledge.

Remind the group that you will ask each couple to share one thing they discovered or discussed during their HomeBuilders Project.

Invite group members to offer one-sentence prayers for continued growth in their prayer lives. Then invite everyone to enjoy a brief time of fellowship and refreshments.

SESSION 4

The Power of Prayer in Marriage

Effective prayer includes praise, confession and supplication.

Begin this session by sharing one thing you learned from **HomeBuilders Project #3**.

I. The Power of Prayer in Marriage

Most of us long for closeness and companionship in our marriages. We may try to fulfill the longing through activities and projects like fixing up the house or taking a trip together; yet when the projects are complete, we often still feel a void.

A. What would happen in a marriage relationship if one partner was not confessing sin to God?

_____

B. How do you think any tendencies toward self-centeredness in your marriage would be affected if you regularly praised God together?

_____

C. How do you think praying together would affect your growth and unity as a couple?

_____

HOMEBUILDERS PRINCIPLE #3:

Praying to God together helps produce the cleansing, forgiveness, humility and unity essential to continued growth in marriage.

D. Do you pray together often as a couple? If so, how do you do it?

_____

How do you fit it into your schedule?

_____

What can you do to make prayer exciting?

_____

II. Basic Components of Prayer

Because prayer is talking with God, it's a wonderful way to develop your relationship with Him. However, many people know little about what to do as they pray.

The Psalms of the Bible are among the best-known and best-loved writings of all literature. Many psalms are actually prayers, and from them we can learn about some basic components of prayer.

A. _Praise_: Psalm 96 illustrates one major component of prayer—praise of God. Praising God means focusing on His character and His deeds and giving Him public acclaim. Read verses 1-10.

1. If you were to spend time consistently praising God, how would that practice affect the way you look at various problems you encounter in life?

   _____

2. What is something you can praise God for right now?

   _____

B. *Confession*: Psalm 51 is treasured as one of the greatest expressions of confession. Read verses 1-13, in which King David confesses his transgressions—committing adultery with Bathsheba and sending her husband off to be killed in battle.
   1. How would you describe the burden David felt because of his sin?

      _____

   2. What did David's confession accomplish?

      _____

   3. Read 1 John 1:9. What happens when you confess a specific sin?

      _____

C. *Supplication*: Psalm 34 is often read and quoted to encourage us to bring our needs and desires to God in prayer. This is called supplication. Read verses 4-18.
   1. What do you find in these verses that would motivate you to pray regularly?

      _____

   2. What does Matthew 7:7-11 have to say about making requests to the Lord?

      _____

Make a date with your mate to meet in the next few days to complete **HomeBuilders Project #4**. This project will help you as a couple to develop a more consistent prayer life.

You'll need to bring a notebook and paper with you when you meet with your mate to complete the **HomeBuilders Project**. Your leader will ask you at the next session to share one experience or insight from your time together.

_____ _____ _____

Date   Time   Location

Recommended Reading

Too Busy Not to Pray, by Bill Hybels.

Most of us have trouble finding time to pray. This book presents a plan for slowing down to be with God.

The Knowledge of the Holy, by A. W. Tozer.

Nothing will have a greater impact on your prayer life than getting to know the One to whom you are praying. This book is a classic guide to that knowledge.

HomeBuilders Project #4

Note: You'll need a notebook with paper to complete question 3 in the "Interact as a Couple" time below.

Individually: 10-15 Minutes

1. Review the entire **Blueprints** section.
2. What are some needs in your life at this time? List them below as prayer requests, then spend some time praying through the list.

_____

3. What are some needs in your mate's life? List them below as prayer requests, then spend some time praying through the list.

_____

Interact as a Couple: 10-15 Minutes

1. Share with each other the insights from your individual time.
2. One tool that can help make prayer meaningful and significant in your life is a prayer journal. In it you enter specific prayer requests or needs and the date. Later, when the prayer is answered, you record the results. Below is a sample format.

Date	Prayer Request	Answer
_____	_____	_____
_____	_____	_____
_____	_____	_____
_____	_____	_____
_____	_____	_____
_____	_____	_____

3. As part of this **HomeBuilders Couples Series®** experience, you'll keep a joint prayer journal for the next few weeks. Doing this will give you a measurable way of seeing God at work in your lives. Few experiences are more exciting!

    In your notebook, list some things you'd like to begin praying for as a couple.

4. Spend a few minutes in prayer together, following the outline of praise, confession and supplication.

Remember to bring your calendar to the next session so you can **Make a Date.**

The Guidebook for Growth

OBJECTIVES

You will help your group members recognize the Bible as a practical and authoritative guide for marriage as you lead them to:

- Consider the value of the Bible as a resource for individuals and couples; and
- Recall experiences in which the Bible has provided specific benefits in their lives.

COMMENTS

Session Five is an unusual Bible study in that the Bible is not just the tool, but also the topic. Called by some "the least read best-seller of all time," the Bible often is ignored by many of the same people who declare its benefits. The key for you as a leader is to show your people how the Bible can actually change their lives. The single most important way to encourage people to get into the Word is for them to have a positive experience using the Word during the session. They may nod their heads in agreement and take wonderful notes about all the good things said about the Bible, but that agreement will have little or no impact unless they open the Scriptures for themselves and seek to learn from them.

Duplicate copies of the Session Five handouts for each class member. Also have Bibles and extra pens or pencils for class members.

Focus

The greatest book ever written is God's gift to help you grow closer to Him and to your mate.

Warm-Up

(15-20 Minutes)

Students are on page 86.

The Warm Up is intended to stimulate interaction, raise interest in the topic and help people make the transition from a busy schedule to a time of discussion and study. Without applying pressure, offer opportunities for some of the quieter members of the group to comment during this time. If a person can enter the flow of a conversation at the beginning, he or she will find it easier to remain involved. However, many people who do not get into the conversation early will find it hard to ever volunteer a comment later on.

Start the session on time, even if everyone is not yet present. Thank group members for their interest and willingness to participate. Divide the class into groups of no more than six per group. Tell one thing you learned from doing HomeBuilders Project #4 this past week. Then ask whichever partner in each couple who watches the most TV to share similarly with their group, telling one thing they learned from their HomeBuilders Project. Affirm group members for having completed the project and encourage those who didn't to complete HomeBuilders Project #5 this coming week.

Share something you learned from *HomeBuilders Project #4*.

Play Bible Trivia.

Tip: *Ask one group at a time to answer one of the trivia questions. Group members can confer for a few seconds, and if they give the right answer, they get a point. If their answer is incorrect, the next group gets to answer. Option: Provide a reward (i.e., chocolate kisses) for the team with the most points.*

1. What is the shortest verse in the Bible?

Answer: "Jesus wept" found in John 11:35.

2. What is the "Great Commission"?

_____

Answer: Jesus' final commandment to His followers, found in Matthew 28:18-20: "And Jesus came up and spoke to them, saying, 'All authority has been given to Me in heaven and on earth. Go therefore and make disciples of all the nations, baptizing them in the name of the Father and the Son and the Holy Spirit, teaching them to observe all that I commanded you; and lo, I am with you always, even to the end of the age.'"

3. How many books are in the Bible?

_____

Answer: 66

4. Recite John 3:16.
5. How many wise men visited the baby Jesus?

_____

Answer: Number is unknown. It's widely believed that there were three because they brought three gifts (see Matthew 2:11), but Scripture doesn't actually say.

6. What is the fourth book in the New Testament?

_____

Answer: The Gospel of John

7. Where was Paul when he wrote the book of Ephesians?

_____

Answer: In prison, probably in Rome (Ephesians 3:1)

8. Who is called the "father of a multitude of nations"?

_____

Answer: Abraham (see Genesis 17:5)

9. Who married David after making a deal which so stunned her husband that he suffered a stroke and died?

_____

Answer: Abigail (see 1 Samuel 25)

10. What did the Apostle Paul call teachers who forbid people to marry?

_____

Answer: "hypocritical liars" (see 1 Timothy 4:2,3, NIV)

(25-35 Minutes)

This section gets couples thinking of the value of the Bible and how they can benefit from knowing that God's Word presents absolute truth for everyday living.

I. The Value of the Bible (15-25 Minutes)

Students are on page 87.

Tip: Read aloud this introductory paragraph and the brief essay on "The Book of Books." Ask class members to follow along on their handouts.

The word Bible simply means "books." Because of the significance and impact of its books, however, the Christian Bible is reverenced as the *Holy Bible.* A brief essay by Henry Van Dyke expresses the value of this timeless treasure to all humankind.

The Book of Books

Born in the East and clothed in Oriental form and imagery, the Bible walks the ways of all the world with familiar feet, and enters land after land to find its own everywhere. It has learned to speak in hundreds of languages to the heart of man. It comes into the palace to tell the monarch that he is a servant of the Most High, and into the cottage to assure the peasant that he is a son of God. Children listen to its stories with wonder and delight and wise men ponder them as parables of life. It has a word of peace for the time of peril, a word of comfort for the time of calamity, a word of light for the hour of darkness. Its oracles are repeated in the assembly of the people, and its counsels whispered in the ear of the lonely.

The wicked and the proud tremble at its warnings, but to the wounded and the penitent it has a mother's voice. The wilderness and the solitary place have been made glad by it, and the fire on the hearth has lit the reading of its well-worn pages. It has woven itself into our dearest dreams; so that love, friendship, sympathy and devotion, memory, and hope put on the beautiful garments of its treasured speech, breathing of frankincense and myrrh.

Henry Van Dyke

Tip: You and your mate share your own responses to question A, focusing on benefits to your marriage relationship. Then invite volunteers to share their answers.

A. From your experience, what benefits have you gained from reading and studying the Bible?

_____

B. Read Psalm 119:160. Why is it so important in today's culture to know that God's Word presents absolute, everlasting truth?

_____

Answer: In today's American culture, the standards for morality are becoming more and more confused. Whereas most Americans once believed that the Bible was the standard for determining right from wrong, many people today believe that each individual should be free to set these standards. As a result, the evidence that immorality and godlessness are quickly increasing is all around us. That's why it's so important to know that "the sum of Thy word is truth, and every one of Thy righteous ordinances is everlasting." God's Word gives us a rock to stand on—a foundation for our lives.

Tip: If your class members don't seem aware of the battle for moral standards that is currently going on in our culture, be prepared to ask a follow-up question such as, "If you were to ask your friends what they base their moral decisions on, what would they be likely to say?"

HOMEBUILDERS PRINCIPLE #4:

The Bible gives couples a solid foundation for making moral and ethical decisions in a godless culture.

C. Another reason the Word of God is such a treasure is that it provides such wonderful personal benefit.

Tip: Point out that Psalm 19 and Psalm 119 are classic expressions of praise for the rich benefits God's Word brings to us. Read aloud Psalm 19:7-11. Then share your own response to question 1 before asking class members to tell their answers.

1. Read Psalm 19:7-11. How have you personally seen the Word of God cause growth by restoring your soul?

_____

Answer: The Word of God renews our perspective so that we can have a new beginning. It points us to the truth and allows us to see God's perspective on various problems we face.

By giving you wisdom?

_____

Answer: The Word of God gives us principles. It gives us objectivity. It gives us wisdom for life. It gives a clear standpoint on what is right and wrong even at times when we may be very confused.

Tip: Ask a class member to read aloud Psalm 119:49,50. Then ask volunteers to respond to question 2.

2. Read Psalm 119:49,50. How does the Word of God give you hope?

_____

Answer: The Word of God helps us see the work of God in history. By remembering how He has worked in the past, we can get a glimpse of how He can work in our lives.

Comfort you in affliction?

_____

Answer: During difficult times, there are many verses in Scripture that can give us strength, insight and peace.

Tip: Ask class members to list as many answers as possible to question D. List them on the chalkboard, flipchart or overhead. Then invite the class to vote for the best answer given. Read aloud HomeBuilders Principle #5.

D. To sum up, why is the Bible so essential if we are to grow as Christians?

_____

Answer: We can't grow without restoration of our soul. We can't grow without hope. We can't grow if we are discouraged. By supplying restoration, hope and encouragement, the Bible supplies the resources we need to grow.

HOMEBUILDERS PRINCIPLE #5:

Couples who place a high value on knowing the Bible will discover the spiritual food their souls need to survive.

Students are on page 88.

II. Evaluating the Bible's Benefits (10 Minutes)

This section helps class members evaluate ways the Bible has benefited them as individuals and as couples.

Tip: Ask each person to silently write his or her answers to the following three questions. After several minutes, invite volunteers to share what they wrote.

A. If you were to begin reading and studying the Bible regularly, how do you think this would affect your life?

_____

B. If you were to begin reading and studying the Bible with your spouse on a regular basis, how do you think this would affect your marriage relationship?

_____

C. How can Scripture help you raise children?

_____

Students are on page 89.

Make a Date

(5 Minutes)

The HomeBuilders Projects are absolutely essential for couples to do together during the week. This week, couples will identify why they may not read the Bible together and plan a schedule for doing this regularly.

Ask everyone to look at the Make a Date section of the handout and then agree with their mates on a time this week to complete HomeBuilders Project #5 together. Encourage couples to set aside 20-30 minutes to respond to the items individually and then discuss their answers together.

Remind the group that at the next session you will ask everyone to share one thing from the HomeBuilders Project as a way of encouraging one another and maintaining accountability with each other.

Make a date with your mate to meet in the next few days to complete *HomeBuilders Project #5.* This project will help you to study the Bible together as a couple. Your leader will ask you at the next session to share one thing from this experience.

Be sure to bring your prayer notebook with you when you meet together to do the *HomeBuilders Project!*

Date	Time	Location

Encourage couples to make use of the resources in the books listed below before the next session.

Manners and Customs of the Bible, by James M. Freeman.

This is a standard reference on the origin and meaning of manners and customs familiar to the authors of the Scriptures.

What the Bible Is All About, by Henrietta C. Mears.

This user-friendly survey of the whole and the parts of the Bible comes complete with outlines and charts that help summarize the vast amount of data in God's Word.

Dismiss in prayer or invite group members to volunteer brief prayers focused on the need to study God's Word together as couples.

Invite everyone to enjoy a time of fellowship and refreshments.

The Guidebook for Growth

The greatest book ever written is God's gift to help you grow closer to Him and to your mate.

Share something you learned from HomeBuilders Project #4.

_____

Blueprints

I. The Value of the Bible

The word Bible simply means "books." Because of the significance and impact of its books, however, the Christian Bible is reverenced as the *Holy Bible*. A brief essay by Henry Van Dyke expresses the value of this timeless treasure to all humankind.

The Book of Books

Born in the East and clothed in Oriental form and imagery, the Bible walks the ways of all the world with familiar feet, and enters land after land to find its own everywhere. It has learned to speak in hundreds of languages to the heart of man. It comes into the palace to tell the monarch that he is a servant of the Most High, and into the cottage to assure the peasant that he is a son of God. Children listen to its stories with wonder and delight and wise men ponder them as parables of life. It has a word of peace for the time of peril, a word of comfort for the time of calamity, a word of light for the hour of darkness. Its oracles are repeated in the assembly of the people, and its counsels whispered in the ear of the lonely.

The wicked and the proud tremble at its warnings, but to the wounded and the penitent it has a mother's voice. The wilderness and the solitary place have been made glad by it, and the fire on the hearth has lit the reading of its well-worn pages. It has woven itself into our dearest dreams; so that love, friendship, sympathy and devotion, memory, and hope put on the beautiful garments of its treasured speech, breathing of frankincense and myrrh.

Henry Van Dyke

A. From your experience, what benefits have you gained from reading and studying the Bible?

_____

B. Read Psalms 119:160. Why is it so important in today's culture to know that God's Word presents absolute, everlasting truth?

_____

HOMEBUILDERS PRINCIPLE #4:

The Bible gives couples a solid foundation for making moral and ethical decisions in a godless culture.

C. Another reason the Word of God is such a treasure is that it provides such wonderful personal benefit.

1. Read Psalm 19:7-11. How have you personally seen the Word of God cause growth by restoring your soul?

   _____

   By giving wisdom?

   _____

2. Read Psalm 119:49,50. How does the Word of God give you hope?

   _____

   Comfort you in affliction?

   _____

D. To sum up, why is the Bible so essential if we are to grow as Christians?

   _____

HOMEBUILDERS PRINCIPLE #5:

Couples who place a high value on knowing the Bible will discover the spiritual food their souls need to survive.

II. Evaluating the Bible's Benefits

A. If you were to begin reading and studying the Bible regularly, how do you think this would affect your life?

   _____

B. If you were to begin reading and studying the Bible with your spouse on a regular basis, how do you think this would affect your marriage relationship?

   _____

C. How can Scripture help you raise children?

   _____

Make a date with your mate to meet in the next few days to complete **HomeBuilders Project #5.** This project will help you discuss your need for studying the Bible together as a couple. Your leader will ask you at the next session to share one thing from this experience.

Be sure to bring your prayer notebook with you when you meet together to do the **HomeBuilders Project!**

Date	Time	Location

Manners and Customs of the Bible, by James M. Freeman.

This is a standard reference on the origin and meaning of manners and customs familiar to the authors of the Scriptures.

What the Bible Is All About, by Henrietta C. Mears.

This user-friendly survey of the whole and the parts of the Bible comes complete with outlines and charts that help summarize the vast amount of data in God's Word.

Individually: 10-15 Minutes

1. Read through the entire **Blueprints** section.
2. Why do you need to be reading the Bible right now, as individuals and as a couple?

   _____

   What needs are driving you to seek the Lord?

   _____

3. What is currently preventing you from spending time in God's Word individually and as a couple?

   _____

Interact as a Couple: 15-30 Minutes

1. Share the work you completed in the individual time. Listen nonjudgmentally.
2. Pull out your prayer notebook and update it, noting any answers to prayer or adding further requests. Finish by praying through your notebook together and asking Him to enable you to deal with the obstacles that get in the way of regular Bible study.

Remember to bring your calendar to the next session so you can **Make a Date.**

SESSION 6

Using Your Guidebook

OBJECTIVES

You will help your group members begin to read the Bible more regularly and productively as you guide them to:

- Discuss some common barriers which hinder couples from regularly studying the Bible; and
- Practice using observation, interpretation and application in the study of the Bible.

COMMENTS

Session Six follows up on the previous session, helping couples to talk openly about some of the typical difficulties people face in making regular Bible study a part of their marriages. The session then moves into explaining and demonstrating an effective plan individuals and couples can use to make their Bible study more productive.

A workable plan for exploring God's Word as a couple will help you grow closer to Him and to your mate.

Students are on page 98.

(15-20 Minutes)

The Warm Up is intended to build relationships while also raising interest in this session's exploration of Bible study barriers and tips.

As people arrive, guide them to form groups of no more than six people per group. Give each group a large blank sheet of paper and three or four felt-tip pens. Assign each group two or three stanzas of Psalm 119. (The chapter is divided into twenty-two eight-verse stanzas. The verses of each stanza begin with the letter of the Hebrew alphabet which heads that stanza.) Instruct the groups to read their stanzas and find one or more descriptions for God's Word. They then make a poster or banner depicting a benefit that reading the Bible provides. **Note:** Many people learn better visually than they do by reading or listening. An activity of this type provides a valuable opportunity for those people, and can stimulate new insights for everyone else as well.

At the official starting time, announce that the session has begun. Allow groups to work another ten minutes or so. Then invite volunteers from each group to show their poster.

You or your mate tell one thing you learned from doing **HomeBuilders Project #5** this past week. Then ask the person in each group who most recently cleaned a bathroom to share similarly from their **HomeBuilders Project** time. Affirm group members for having completed the project and encourage any others to make a renewed effort to do so this coming week.

Share something you learned from *HomeBuilders Project #5*.

(25-35 Minutes)

*This session's **Blueprints** uncovers some barriers to regular Bible study for couples and then introduces some effective approaches to Bible study.*

I. Overcoming Barriers to Studying the Bible (10 Minutes)

Students are on page 98.

A. What are some obstacles that keep you from studying the Bible consistently as an individual?

_____

Possible Answers: No plan. No time. No interest. No quiet place for study. Also, some people may feel overwhelmed by the breadth of the Bible.

Tip: Briefly mention one obstacle that has interfered with consistent Bible study in your personal life and in your marriage. Then instruct the groups to work together for a few minutes to compile a list of barriers they have encountered. After two or three minutes, call on someone in each group who has not spoken aloud very often in the class, asking them to share one or two barriers mentioned in their group.

As a couple?

_____

Possible Answers: Many of the same reasons apply: no plan, no time. Another reason may be that some married partners have neglected their spiritual development as a couple and have no commitment to grow together in Christ. Both partners may be hesitant to encourage studying the Bible together, being worried about how their mate will respond.

B. **If you have studied the Bible together as a couple, how have you done it?**

_____

What has worked for you?

_____

Possible Answers: Typically, couples who experience success in studying the Bible together mention making a commitment to each other to work together at it, setting aside a specific time on a regular basis, establishing a definite plan of what to study and seeking to apply what they read to their marriage relationship.

Tip: Share one or two things you and your mate have done which have been helpful in your mutual study times. Then invite class members to share their experiences.

Students are on page 99.

II. An Approach to Studying the Bible (15-25 Minutes)

Tip: Point out that there are many ways people have gone about studying the Bible. The rest of this session explores one Bible study approach that has proven effective for a great many people. Ask everyone to locate 2 Timothy 2:15. Then ask a class member to read the verse aloud. Invite volunteers to answer question A.

A. Read 2 Timothy 2:15. Why is it important to "handle accurately the word of truth"?

_____

Answer: The biggest reason is that if we don't know how to handle the Word of God accurately, we may misinterpret it. Many of today's cults base their ideas on misinterpreted Bible passages. In addition, accurately handling the Word is part of presenting ourselves to God as "approved workmen," we don't want to feel shame because we have such a poor working knowledge of the Scriptures. Finally, in a day of trivial pursuits and inconsequential goals, having an accurate perception of the Word of God gives wisdom and authority to our life.

Tip: Assign each of the groups one of the three steps to effective Bible study. The group members are to work together to write a statement that, in 25 words or less, explains why their assigned step is beneficial. After three or four minutes, call on someone from each group to read their statement aloud.

B. There are many different methods of Bible study which help you handle the Word accurately. One basic procedure which many people enjoy involves the following three steps:

Step One: *Observe* the parts of speech, word relationships and other basic facts about the passage you're studying. The object of this step is to answer the question "What do I see here?"

Step Two: *Interpret* the passage. The object here is to figure out what the passage means. Ask yourself such questions as, "Why did the author say this? To whom was he speaking? What problem was he addressing?"

Step Three: *Apply* what you have learned by determining what difference this truth can make in your life right now.

Comment on Step Three: Too many people know what the Bible says but they don't act upon that knowledge. Without application we never use the principles and insights of the Word. Also, we lose enthusiasm for further study if we aren't experiencing the challenge and joy of seeing God's Word make a difference in our lives.

II. An Approach to Studying the Bible

Tip: *Share an illustration from your own study of how these steps have been mean-ingful for you. Then lead the groups in working together to use these steps in study-ing two verses in Philippians.*

C. Using this method, let's do a brief Bible study on Philippians 4:6,7. Begin by read-ing the passage twice, slowly and carefully. Then proceed with the three steps:

Tip: *Allow about ten minutes for groups to read and discuss the Scripture, sharing first their observations, then their interpretations and finally their applications. Keep the groups aware of the time remaining, encouraging them to keep moving so they are able to deal with all three steps. Announce when time is up and have the groups pray together to conclude their study. Then ask for volunteers to share with the class their answers to the questions on their handouts.*

1. Step One: *Observe.*

    a. What is the main idea of this passage?

    _____

Answer: *There is a cause-and-effect connection between verses 6 and 7. If we meet the conditions described in verse 6, we will have the fruit we see in verse 7.*

    b. What are some of the key words?

    _____

Answer: *Key words include "anxiety", "everything" and "requests".*

2. Step Two: *Interpret.*

    a. What does it mean to be "anxious for nothing"?

    _____

Answer: *When we are anxious about something, our anxiety means we aren't trust-ing God to take care of the situation. We are carrying the burden of it rather than giv-ing that burden to Christ. When we are "anxious for nothing," we still may have to take action on the problem, but we are looking for God to provide the real solution.*

    b. What does it mean to pray about "everything"?

    _____

Answer: *"Everything" means everything. We should not exclude anything from our prayers, God is interested in every area of our lives.*

    c. How does the peace of God surpass "all comprehension"?

    _____

Answer: God's peace is more than we can understand, it is supernatural. Even in the midst of horrible circumstances, God's peace is available if we trust in Him.

> **d.** How does praying to God give you this peace?
>
> _____

Answer: It's the first step of releasing our anxieties to Him so that His peace can flood our souls.

3. Step Three: *Apply.*

> **a.** Have you ever experienced God's peace after you prayed about a situation you were anxious about? Tell about the experience if you can.
>
> _____

Tip: Be ready to share an experience of your own here. You may be able to prompt discussion by suggesting possible situations where people experience anxiousness (for instance, sickness in the family, strained relationships or problems at work).

> **b.** What are some situations you are anxious about right now?
>
> _____
>
> **c.** Spend a few minutes in prayer right now about these situations and ask for God's guidance and peace.

Tip: Read aloud HomeBuilders Principle #6 to summarize this session.

HOMEBUILDERS PRINCIPLE #6:

It is possible to become a Christian with little Bible knowledge, but it is impossible to grow together in Christ without regular study of the Scriptures.

Students are on page 100.

(5 Minutes)

This week's HomeBuilders Project will help couples plan a schedule for regular Bible study.
    Ask everyone to look at the Make a Date section of the handout, then agree with their mate on a time this week to complete HomeBuilders Project #6 together. Encourage couples

to set aside 20-30 minutes to respond to the items individually and then discuss their answers together.

Remind the group that at the next session you will ask everyone to share one thing from the HomeBuilders Project as a way of encouraging one another and maintaining account-ability with each other.

Make a date with your mate to meet in the next few days to complete *HomeBuilders Project #6*. This project will help you to study the Bible together as a couple. Your leader will ask you at the next session to share one thing from this experience.

Be sure to bring your prayer notebook with you when you meet together to do the *HomeBuilders Project!*

_____	_____	_____
Date	Time	Location

Encourage couples to make use of the resources in the books listed below before the next session.

Simply Understanding the Bible, by Irving Jensen.

This resource includes a quick overview of each book of the Bible, commentary on key New Testament passages and pertinent Bible-times maps.

The Joy of Teaching Discovery Bible Study, by Oletta Wald.

Here is a time-honored workbook and guide for grasping the author's intent and the structure of each book of the Bible.

Dismiss in prayer or invite group members to volunteer brief prayers focused on the need to study God's Word together as couples.

Invite everyone to enjoy a time of fellowship and refreshments.

Using Your Guidebook

A workable plan for exploring God's Word as a couple will help you grow closer to Him and to your mate.

Share something you learned from HomeBuilders Project #5.

I. Overcoming Barriers to Studying the Bible

A. What are some obstacles that keep you from studying the Bible consistently as an individual?

_____

As a couple?

_____

B. If you have studied the Bible together as a couple, how have you done it?

_____

What has worked for you?

_____

II. An Approach to Studying the Bible

A. Read 2 Timothy 2:15. Why is it important to "handle accurately the word of truth"?

_____

B. There are many different methods of Bible study which help you handle the Word accurately. One basic procedure which many people enjoy involves the following three steps:

Step One: *Observe* the parts of speech, word relationships and other basic facts about the passage you're studying. The object of this step is to answer the question "What do I see here?"

Step Two: *Interpret* the passage. The object here is to figure out what the passage means. Ask yourself such questions as, "Why did the author say this? To whom was he speaking? What problem was he addressing?"

Step Three: *Apply* what you have learned by determining what difference this truth can make in your life right now.

C. Using this method, let's do a brief Bible study on Philippians 4:6,7. Begin by reading the passage twice, slowly and carefully. Then proceed with the three steps:

1. Step One: *Observe.*
    a. What is the main idea of this passage?

    _____

    b. What are some of the key words?

    _____

2. Step Two: *Interpret.*
    a. What does it mean to be "anxious for nothing"?

    _____

    b. What does it mean to pray about "everything"?

    _____

    c. How does the peace of God surpass "all comprehension"?

    _____

    d. How does praying to God give you this peace?

    _____

3. Step Three: *Apply.*
    a. Have you ever experienced God's peace after you prayed about a situation you were anxious about? Tell about the experience, if you can.

    _____

    b. What are some situations you are anxious about right now?

    _____

c. Spend a few minutes in prayer right now about these situations and ask for God's guidance and peace.

HOMEBUILDERS PRINCIPLE #6:

It is possible to become a Christian with little Bible knowledge, but it is impossible to grow together in Christ without regular study of the Scriptures.

Make a date with your mate to meet in the next few days to complete **HomeBuilders Project #6**. This project will help you to study the Bible together as a couple. Your leader will ask you at the next session to share one thing from this experience.

Be sure to bring your prayer notebook with you when you meet together to do the **HomeBuilders Project!**

| _____ | _____ | _____ |
| Date | Time | Location |

Simply Understanding the Bible, by Irving Jensen.

This resource includes a quick overview of each book of the Bible, commentary on key New Testament passages and pertinent Bible-times maps.

The Joy of Teaching Discovery Bible Study, by Oletta Wald.

Here is a time-honored workbook and guide for grasping the author's intent and the structure of each book of the Bible.

Individually: 10-15 Minutes

1. Read through the entire **Blueprints** section.
2. Rough out a plan for reading and studying the Bible together regularly. There are numerous possible approaches to studying the Bible; here are just a few to get you started:

Reading Programs
- Read through five chapters of Psalms and one chapter of Proverbs each day. In a month you'll have completed both books.
- Read through three chapters of the Gospel of John each day. You'll complete it four times in less than 30 days.
- Read through one chapter of the Gospels each day.

Study Programs
- Explore different books of the Bible. Pick a book, preferably a short one to start with, and read through it several times noting themes and favorite verses. Use the "Observe, Interpret, Apply" formula described in the **Blueprints** section.
- Examine the lives and experiences of people in the Bible. Choose a character you are interested in—Joseph, Daniel, Esther, Apollos, etc. Find all the verses and passages in which this character appears or is mentioned. Look for clues to the character's personality, his or her strengths, weaknesses and motivations. Look for ways to apply this person's experiences to your own life.
- Study key words in the Bible. Choose a word such as "peace" or "humility" and using a Bible concordance, look up verses in which the word appears.

Interact as a Couple: 10-15 Minutes

1. Share the work you completed in the individual time. Listen nonjudgmentally, being alert for how you can complement your spouse in building or rebuilding your time in the Word individually and together.
2. Decide together upon a specific plan—including a definite schedule—for how you'll start studying the Bible together as a couple.
3. Finish by praying together and committing your plans and purposes to the Lord. Look to Him to enable you to achieve success in this area for growing together in Christ.

Remember to bring your calendar to the next session so you can **Make a Date**.

The Holy Spirit: Your Partner in Marriage

OBJECTIVES

You will help your class members identify ways the Holy Spirit can help their marriages as you guide them to:

- Recognize their need for divine power in living the Christian life; and
- Discuss Bible passages on what the Holy Spirit does within the life of the Christian.

COMMENTS

The content of this session is pivotal in the life of any Christian. It is the Holy Spirit who gives us the power to live a life pleasing to God. If we attempt to live the Christian life in our own power without the Spirit, we end up frustrated and defeated.

For some in your group, recognizing the work of the Holy Spirit will bring totally new enlightenment. Others may know about the Holy Spirit but may need to personally apply that knowledge. Still others may need to make a recommitment by being filled once again with the Spirit.

Be in prayer before this session that each man and woman will be receptive to the Holy Spirit's gentle persuasion in his or her life.

The Holy Spirit is available to enable any Christian couple to experience God's best within their marriage.

Students are on page 110.

(10-15 Minutes)

The Warm Up section gets people interacting about their need for the power of the Holy Spirit rather than trying to live the Christian life in their own power.

Start the session on time, even if everyone is not yet present. Tell one thing you learned from doing HomeBuilders Project #6 this past week. Ask for a show of hands of the couples who also completed the project. Commend them and call on several who responded, asking them to tell one thing they learned through doing the project on Bible reading.

1. Share something you learned in *HomeBuilders Project #6*.

Tip: Read aloud the case study as class members follow along on their handouts. Invite responses to the question at the end of the case study.

2. Read the following case study:

In the two years since Dan and Nancy received Christ as their Savior, they've seen their lifestyle change dramatically. They have begun to study the Bible regularly. Occasionally, in fact, they rise early to make sure they can read God's Word and pray together before their busy day begins.

You'll find Dan and Nancy at church every Sunday morning with bright smiles on their faces. Nancy sings in the choir, and they both attend Sunday School. Dan has even volunteered to go with the junior high group on an overnight camping trip.

But, even though Dan and Nancy appear to be model young believers, lately they have confessed to a certain frustration in their spiritual lives. The joy is fading. At times it seems like they're just going through the motions with all these Christian activities, and the activities are beginning to seem boring. They also feel powerless when they think of telling their friends and neighbors about knowing the Lord. For all their efforts, they do not really feel close to God, and they don't have any sense of His presence and power.

What do you think is Nancy and Dan's problem?

Answer: Dan and Nancy seem to be focused on living the Christian life on their own power, not by drawing power from the Lord. Many Christians fall into this same trap: They know there are all kinds of things they should be doing on a regular basis— praying, reading the Bible, ministering to others, witnessing, etc.—but they have little idea of how to tap into the power of the Holy Spirit. The Christian life becomes just another series of activities as they try to achieve spiritual vitality through their own efforts.

(30-40 Minutes)

This Blueprints section helps people recognize their need for spiritual power and understand how the Holy Spirit works in us.

I. The Need for Spiritual Power
(10-15 Minutes)

Students are on page 111.

Tip: Divide the class into groups of two or three. Couples can work together if they desire. Allow two minutes for people to share with each other their answers to question A, with each group seeking to list as many things about the Holy Spirit as they can within the time limit.

When the two minutes are up, invite volunteers to share with the class the answers they gave.

A. If someone were to ask you "What is the Holy Spirit?", how would you answer him or her from what you know right now?

_____

Answer: The correct answer, of course, is that the Holy Spirit is fully God, the third person of the Trinity, who lives in each believer today. Many Christians, though, are uninformed about the Holy Spirit, and you may hear some fuzzy responses to this question.

Tip: If you sense confusion or uncertainty in your group about who the Holy Spirit is, or if any are silent and don't know how to answer the question, use that response as a springboard into the remainder of the lesson. Comment that this confusion and silence proves how real the problem is. Christians often don't understand who the Holy Spirit is.

B. Why do you think so few Christians understand the ministry of the Holy Spirit?

_____

Answer: Many people have never been clearly taught about the Holy Spirit, and they have never studied what the Bible says about the Spirit.

Tip: Have everyone locate 2 Peter 1:3. Ask a class member to read it aloud, then ask for responses to question C.

C. Read 2 Peter 1:3. What could you as a couple be missing if you try to live the Christian life in your own power?

_____

Answer: We could be missing the divine power that allows us to live a godly life. In other words, we would really have a substandard Christian life.

II. The Holy Spirit at Work in Us
(20-25 Minutes)

Students are on page 111.

Tip: Assign all the wives to look up and read John 14:16,17 while the husbands do the same with 2 Timothy 1:14. Allow a minute or so for people to read, then ask for responses to question A.

A. What do the following verses have to say about your relationship with the Holy Spirit?

1. John 14:16,17

_____

Answer: The Holy Spirit is "another helper," someone like Jesus. He is sent to be with us forever. Notice the descriptions used in these two verses: first, He "may be with you" (v. 16) and He "will be in you" (v. 17). These indicate that our relationships with the Holy Spirit are meant to be very intimate ones.

2. 2 Timothy 1:14

_____

Answer: This verse reinforces the same truth, stating that the Holy Spirit dwells within us.

B. The Holy Spirit enters your life when you invite Jesus Christ to be your Savior and Master, but many people are ignorant of what the Holy Spirit can do for a Christian each day. What do the following verses reveal?

Tip: Divide the class into thirds. Assign everyone in each third to look up one of the references in question B. Have people meet in the same groups of two or three to discuss their answers to the question. After several minutes, call on several people in each section to share their answers with the class.

1. John 16:13-15

_____

Answer: The Holy Spirit is our guide to truth. He helps us understand the Scripture, and He also discloses the will of God to us.

2. Acts 1:8

_____

Answer: In this verse, Jesus states that the Holy Spirit will be our source of power to be witnesses to all the world. Notice that Jesus gives the command in the same breath that He mentions the power; He knows we cannot tell others about Christ without the power of the Holy Spirit.

3. Romans 8:26,27

_____

Answer: The Holy Spirit helps us in prayer by interceding for us.

Tip: Lead the class in reading aloud this HomeBuilders Principle:

HOMEBUILDERS PRINCIPLE #7:

The growing Christian life is the Spirit-filled life. The Holy Spirit provides the power you need to obey God on a daily basis.

Tip: Have everyone turn to Galatians 5. Read aloud verses 16-21, then guide the class in discussing questions 1 and 2. Be prepared to share an incident or two from your own marriage in answering question 2. When responding to this question, remind the class of the first ground rule for this class: "Share nothing about your marriage which may embarrass your mate."

C. Read Galatians 5:16-21.

1. What are the results of walking in the power of the flesh?

_____

Answer: Paul lists 15 items here which describe very specifically what our lives are like when we are not drawing on the power of the Spirit, that is, when we are drawing on the power of the flesh. These results include immorality, impurity, sensuality, etc.

2. How have the "deeds of the flesh" (such as those listed in verses 19-21) caused problems in your marriage?

_____

Answer: The deeds of the flesh can cause problems in the sexual area, the communication area and in almost every other aspect of a relationship. These deeds of the flesh attack the couple and set in motion the process to destroy their relationship. People who are controlled by the flesh desire only to please themselves, not their mates.

Tip: Ask for a volunteer to read aloud verses 22 and 23. Then invite responses to question 1.

D. Now read verses 22 and 23 in Galatians 5.

1. What are the results of walking in the power of the Spirit?

_____

Answer: If we're controlled by the Spirit, we'll experience the spiritual fruit that these verses mention. This, in turn, will produce harmony in our marriages, as we seek to please each other.

Tip: Instruct husbands and wives to take several minutes and privately write their responses to question 2 or 3. You and your mate should be prepared to share your own responses to the questions to help encourage people to be honest in their answers.

2. Husbands: Which of these "fruit of the Spirit" characteristics would your wife like to see evident in your life, and how would that fruitfulness help your marriage?

———————————————————————————————

3. Wives: Which of these "fruit of the Spirit" characteristics would your husband like to see evident in your life, and how would that fruitfulness help your marriage?

———————————————————————————————

Tip: If your class has established an open climate of trustful sharing, invite volunteers to share one item they wrote. Point out that one person's sharing can be very helpful to others, encouraging each other in identifying specific ways in which growth is desired.

Lead the class in reading aloud HomeBuilders Principle #8.

HOMEBUILDERS PRINCIPLE #8:
A Christian couple will grow and experience true oneness in marriage by the presence and power of the Holy Spirit.

Students are on page 113.

(5 Minutes)

This week, as they work through the HomeBuilders Project, couples will review what the work of the Holy Spirit is and how to apply what they have learned.

Ask everyone to look at the Make a Date section of the handout, then agree with their mates on a time this week to complete HomeBuilders Project #7 together. Encourage couples to set aside 20-30 minutes to respond to the items individually and then discuss their answers together.

Remind the group that at the next session you will ask everyone to share one thing from the HomeBuilders Project as a way to keep encouraging one another and maintaining accountability with each other.

Make a date with your mate to meet in the next few days to complete *HomeBuilders Project #7.*

Be sure to bring your prayer notebook with you when you meet together to do the *HomeBuilders Project!*

Date	Time	Location

Encourage couples to locate this book and to read all or part of it before the next session.
The Secret, by Bill Bright.

This is the life message of the man used by God to enhance the spiritual walk of literally tens of thousands of Christians.

Dismiss in prayer or invite group members to volunteer brief prayers asking for awareness of the Holy Spirit's presence in their lives and marriages.

Invite everyone to enjoy a time of fellowship and refreshments.

SESSION 7

The Holy Spirit: Your Partner in Marriage

Focus

The Holy Spirit is available to enable any Christian couple to experience God's best within their marriage.

Warm-Up

1. Share something you learned in HomeBuilders Project #6.

2. Read the following case study:

> In the two years since Dan and Nancy received Christ as their Savior, they've seen their lifestyle change dramatically. They have begun to study the Bible regularly. Occasionally, in fact, they rise early to make sure they can read God's Word and pray together before their busy day begins.
>
> You'll find Dan and Nancy at church every Sunday morning with bright smiles on their faces. Nancy sings in the choir, and they both attend Sunday School. Dan has even volunteered to go with the junior high group on an overnight camping trip.

But, even though Dan and Nancy appear to be model young believers, lately they have confessed to a certain frustration in their spiritual lives. The joy is fading. At times it seems like they're just going through the motions with all these Christian activities, and the activities are beginning to seem boring. They also feel powerless when they think of telling their friends and neighbors about knowing the Lord. For all their efforts, they do not really feel close to God, and they don't have any sense of His presence and power.

What do you think is Nancy and Dan's problem?

_____

I. The Need for Spiritual Power

A. If someone were to ask you "What is the Holy Spirit?", how would you answer him or her from what you know right now?
_____

B. Why do you think so few Christians understand the ministry of the Holy Spirit?
_____

C. Read 2 Peter 1:3. What could you as a couple be missing if you try to live the Christian life in your own power?
_____

II. The Holy Spirit at Work in Us

A. What do the following verses have to say about your relationship with the Holy Spirit?
1. John 14:16,17
_____

2. 2 Timothy 1:14
_____

B. The Holy Spirit enters your life when you invite Jesus Christ to be your Savior and Master, but many people are ignorant of what the Holy Spirit can do for a Christian each day. What do the following verses reveal?

1. John 16:13-15
_____

2. Acts 1:8
_____

3. Romans 8:26,27
_____

HOMEBUILDERS PRINCIPLE #7:

The growing Christian life is the Spirit-filled life. The Holy Spirit provides the power you need to obey God on a daily basis.

C. Read Galatians 5:16-21.
   1. What are the results of walking in the power of the flesh?
   _____

   2. How have you seen the "deeds of the flesh" (such as those listed in verses 19-21) cause problems in your marriage?
   _____

D. Now read verses 22 and 23 in Galatians 5.
   1. What are the results of walking in the power of the Spirit?
   _____

   2. Husbands: Which of these "fruit of the Spirit" characteristics would your wife like to see evident in your life, and how would that fruitfulness help your marriage?
   _____

   3. Wives: Which of these "fruit of the Spirit" characteristics would your husband like to see evident in your life, and how would that fruitfulness help your marriage?
   _____

HOMEBUILDERS PRINCIPLE #8:

A Christian couple will grow and experience true oneness in marriage by the presence and power of the Holy Spirit.

Make a date with your mate to meet in the next few days to complete **HomeBuilders Project #7.**

Be sure to bring your prayer notebook with you when you meet together to do the **HomeBuilders Project!**

_____   _____   _____
            Date   Time   Location

The Secret, by Bill Bright.

This is the life message of the man used by God to enhance the spiritual walk of literally tens of thousands of Christians.

Individually: 10-15 Minutes

1. Read through the entire **Blueprints** section.
2. In what areas of your life do you need God's strength and power?

   _____

   What are some areas of difficulty or frustration for you?

   _____

Interact as a Couple: 10-15 Minutes

1. Share with each other your responses and insights from the individual time.
2. Read Ephesians 5:18-21 to each other. While your spouse reads, pray that the Lord will increasingly fulfill these words in your marriage.
3. Pull out your prayer notebook and update it, noting any answers to prayer or adding further requests. Finish by praying through your notebook together and committing your plans and purposes to the Lord. Look to Him to enable you to achieve success in this area for growing together in Christ.

Remember to bring your calendar to the next session so you can **Make a Date**.

SESSION 8

How to Be Filled with the Holy Spirit

OBJECTIVES

You will help your class members begin to live the Christian life in the power of the Holy Spirit as you guide them to:

- Evaluate whether they are currently walking in the Spirit or the flesh; and
- Experience being filled with the Holy Spirit.

COMMENTS

Information about the Holy Spirit cannot be neatly filed away until a more convenient time. Awareness of the Holy Spirit's presence and purpose brings any Christian to a moment of personal decision. The impact of this session will come not so much from your mastery of the content and procedures as from the Holy Spirit personally dealing with each person.

Continue to pray before this session that each man and woman will be receptive to the Holy Spirit's gentle persuasion in his or her life.

Materials Needed:
- a felt-tip pen;
- masking tape;
- 24 strips of colored paper, at least three inches high on which you write one of the works of the flesh and fruit of the Spirit from Galatians 5:19-23;
- two different colors of small sticky notes, enough for each class member to have three or four of both colors.

The Christian couple who draws upon God's power
through the Holy Spirit will experience
growth in their lives.

*Students are on
page 121.*

(10-15 Minutes)

The Warm Up section gets people interacting about how to tap into the power of the Holy Spirit and not live their Christian life on their own power.

Before class write each of the works of the flesh and the fruit of the Spirit from Galatians 5:19-23 on the separate strips of colored paper. Tape the strips to the four walls of the classroom, intermixing those from the two lists.

As people arrive, greet each person warmly and give them three or four of each of the two colors of small sticky notes. Instruct them to check out the actions and attitudes mounted on the walls. They are to attach their sticky notes to those actions and attitudes that they or their mates exhibited during the past week. Explain "Use the (blue) notes to mark actions and attitudes you exhibited. The (yellow) notes are for actions and attitudes you saw in your mate."

When everyone is finished, have a few people share why they placed their sticky notes where they did. Ask them to share specific ways their mates exhibited the fruit of the Spirit.

Once most people have attached their sticky notes, do a quick survey of whether more notes were attached to positive or negative attributes, and whether people tended to see more positive attributes in themselves (blue) or their mates (yellow).

Tell one thing you learned from doing HomeBuilders Project #7 this past week. Ask for a show of hands of the couples who also completed the project. Commend them and call on several who responded, asking them to tell one thing they learned through doing the project on the Holy Spirit.

Share something you learned in *HomeBuilders Project #7*.

(25-35 Minutes)

In this Blueprints section, couples will study Scripture verses to learn how to be filled with the Holy Spirit.

I. Evaluating My Walk
(10-15 Minutes)

Students are on page 122.

Comment: *"Last session we began looking at the Holy Spirit's work in our lives. Today, we are going to expand that study."*

Tip: *Instruct everyone to locate Galatians 5 and silently read verses 16-23. Then have everyone work individually to write their answers to questions A and B.*

Take a few minutes to reread Galatians 5:16-23.

A. As you look at your life during the last few months, do you think you've been walking mostly by the flesh or by the Spirit?

_____

B. As a result of this pattern, how would you characterize your lifestyle?

_____

Tip: *Share your own answers to these questions, briefly describing what your lifestyle was like at a time when you walked mostly by the flesh, and then describing your present walk.*

Then, if your class has established an open, trusting climate with each other, invite volunteers to share their answers to the questions. If you sense at least some people will be reluctant to share their answers, ask, "What evidence have you seen in your life or that of others that walking in the Spirit truly makes a positive difference in daily living?"

Next, ask everyone to silently write their answers to question C.

Students are on page 122.

C. What place do you think the Holy Spirit has had in your marriage up to now?

II. How to Be Filled with the Holy Spirit (15-20 Minutes)

Tip: Lead the class in looking up and reading the Scriptures in this section, inviting volunteers to answer the questions as you come to them.

Three important verses provide the key to understanding how to be filled with the Spirit.

A. Whenever you have sinned, it's safe to say that the Holy Spirit was not filling your life. According to 1 John 1:9, what do you need to do after you have sinned?

Answer: We must confess our sins.

B. Read 1 John 5:14,15. What is the type of prayer that you know will be answered?

How can you know you are praying that kind of prayer?

Answer: This verse promises that God will answer anything we ask "according to His will." And the best way to know His will is to know what Scripture says. If we know that something is God's will, we can be assured that He will answer that prayer. Example: If we pray for a new car, we can't be assured that God will answer that prayer because Scripture gives no definite indication that a new car is part of God's will for us. But if we pray that God will give us His peace during a difficult circumstance, we can be assured that He will do so because of His promise in Philippians 4:6,7.

C. Now read Ephesians 5:18. Keeping the 1 John 5:14,15 passage in mind, how can you know that God will answer your prayer to be filled with His Spirit?

Answer: We already know that God will answer any prayer which is "according to His will." Since you are commanded in Ephesians 5:18 to "be filled with the Spirit," you know it is definitely God's will that you be filled. Therefore, when you pray to be filled with the Spirit, you can be assured that God will answer that prayer.

Tip: Read aloud the explanation in point D of how to become a Spirit-filled husband or wife. If you can, share how you have prayed similar prayers to allow God to control your life through His Holy Spirit. Then read the suggested prayers aloud and invite those who desire to be filled with the Holy Spirit to repeat it in their hearts.

D. Becoming a Spirit-filled husband and wife involves the following two steps:

    1. Step One: As directed in 1 John 1:9, *confess to God whatever sins may be filling and defiling your life. Turn from the sins.*

Dear Father, I acknowledge that I have been in control of my life; and that as a result, I have sinned against You. I thank You that You have forgiven my sins through Christ's death on the cross for me.

    2. Step Two: *Claim, by faith, God's promise to fill you with the Holy Spirit.* Here's a suggested prayer:

Father in heaven, fill me with the Holy Spirit as Your Word directs. Take Your place on the throne of my life; make me into the person You desire me to be. In Jesus' name, amen.

III. Personal Reflections (1-2 Minutes)

Students are on page 123.

Tip: Ask everyone to spend a minute or two reflecting on this session. Then invite volunteers to respond to items A and B.

A. Look back over this session and share the idea, thought or principle which means the most to you.

_____

B. How would marriages be different if both spouses were filled with the Holy Spirit?

_____

Students are on page 123.

(5 Minutes)

This week, as they work through the HomeBuilders Project, couples will review how a person can be filled with the Holy Spirit and walk in the power of the Holy Spirit every day.

Ask everyone to look at the Make a Date section of the handout, then agree with their mates on a time this week to complete HomeBuilders Project #8 together. Encourage couples to set aside 45-60 minutes to respond to the items individually and then discuss their answers together.

Remind the group that at the next session you will ask everyone to share one thing from the HomeBuilders Project as a way of encouraging one another and maintaining accountability with each other.

Make a date with your mate to meet in the next few days to complete *HomeBuilders Project #8.*

Be sure to bring your prayer notebook with you when you meet together to do the *HomeBuilders Project!*

Date	Time	Location

Encourage couples to locate this book and to read all or part of it before the next session.
***The Green Letters**, by Miles J. Stanford.*

This classic devotional study of the principles of spiritual growth is the first book in a series on the distinctive Christian life.

Dismiss in prayer or invite group members to volunteer brief prayers asking for awareness of the Holy Spirit's presence in their lives and marriages.

Invite everyone to enjoy a time of fellowship and refreshments.

SESSION 8

How to Be Filled with the Holy Spirit

Focus

The Christian couple who draws upon God's power through the Holy Spirit will experience growth in their lives.

Warm-Up

Share something you learned in HomeBuilders Project #7.

I. Evaluating My Walk

Take a few minutes to reread Galatians 5:16-23.

A. As you look at your life during the last few months, do you think you've been walking mostly by the flesh or by the Spirit?

_____

B. As a result of this pattern, how would you characterize your lifestyle?

_____

C. What place do you think the Holy Spirit has had in your marriage up to now?

_____

II. How to Be Filled with the Holy Spirit

Three important verses provide the key to understanding how to be filled with the Spirit.

A. Whenever you have sinned, it's safe to say that the Holy Spirit was not filling your life. According to 1 John 1:9, what do you need to do after you have sinned?

_____

B. Read 1 John 5:14,15. What is the type of prayer that you know will be answered?

_____

How can you know you are praying that kind of prayer?

_____

C. Now read Ephesians 5:18. Keeping the 1 John 5:14,15 passage in mind, how can you know that God will answer your prayer to be filled with His Spirit?

_____

D. Becoming a Spirit-filled husband and wife involves the following two steps:

1. Step One: As directed in 1 John 1:9, confess to God whatever sins may be filling and defiling your life. Turn from the sins.

Dear Father, I acknowledge that I have been in control of my life; and that, as a result, I have sinned against You. I thank You that You have forgiven my sins through Christ's death on the cross for me.

2. Step Two: Claim, by faith, God's promise to fill you with the Holy Spirit. Here's a suggested prayer:

Father in heaven, fill me with the Holy Spirit as Your Word directs. Take Your place on the throne of my life; make me into the person You desire me to be. In Jesus' name, amen.

III. Personal Reflections

A. Look back over this session and share the idea, thought or principle which means the most to you.

_____

B. How would marriages be different if both spouses were filled with the Holy Spirit?

_____

Make a date with your mate to meet in the next few days to complete **HomeBuilders Project #8.**

Be sure to bring your prayer notebook with you when you meet together to do the **HomeBuilders Project!**

_____   _____   _____
Date   Time   Location

The Green Letters, by Miles J. Stanford.

This classic devotional study of the principles of spiritual growth is the first book in a series on the distinctive Christian life.

Individually: 10-15 Minutes

1. Read through the entire **Blueprints** section.

2. In addition to learning how to be filled with the Spirit, it's important to learn how to walk in the Spirit on a daily basis.

   a. How can you know when you need to restore your walk with the Lord?

   _____

   b. The process of walking in the Spirit is one of continually yielding to His control in your life. Bill Bright, founder and president of Campus Crusade for Christ, calls this process "spiritual breathing":

      1. *Exhale*: Confess, according to 1 John 1:9, the sin that has broken your stride.
      2. *Inhale*: Pray to be filled freshly with the Holy Spirit, and thank the Lord for the renewal of His powerful presence in your life.

      What are some daily situations in which you could regularly apply this principle?

   _____

3. What can your mate do to encourage you to be filled with the Holy Spirit?

   _____

   Is there anything that he or she does that discourages you?

   _____

Interact as a Couple: 10-15 Minutes

1. Share with each other your responses and insights from the individual time.

2. Discuss your answers from question 3 in the individual time. Make a list together of ways you can encourage and discourage one another to be empowered by the Holy Spirit.

Encourage	Discourage
_____	_____
_____	_____
_____	_____
_____	_____
_____	_____

3. Finish by praying together and committing your plans and purposes to the Lord. Look to Him to enable you to achieve success in this area for growing together in Christ.

Remember to bring your calendar to the next session so you can **Make a Date.**

SESSION 9

The Call to Discipleship

OBJECTIVES

You will help your group members deepen their commitment to live as disciples of Jesus as you guide them to:

- Examine the biblical explanation of the responsibilities, costs and disciplines of discipleship; and
- Explore some of the barriers to and benefits of a life of discipleship.

COMMENTS

This session and the three which follow are the most challenging of the entire study. Whereas past sessions focused on different disciplines of the Christian life, these final sessions will encourage your group members to commit their entire lives to following Christ.

Those in your group who have come to grips with the work of the Holy Spirit in their lives will welcome the practical help provided in this session. Those who still struggle with surrendering their own will to that of the Spirit will also benefit from the insights this session brings to the implications of being a follower of Jesus. Those whose Christianity consists of casually aligning themselves with some of Jesus' teaching, but who have not come to grips with the realities of Christ's claim on their lives, definitely need the straightforward declarations this study provides.

Growing together in Christ means considering both the call and the cost of discipleship.

Students are on page 132.

(10-15 Minutes)

This **Warm Up** *is intended to lead directly to the content of the* **Blueprints** *section which introduces the concept of discipleship.*

As people arrive, greet each person and encourage friendly interaction among class members. When it is time to begin the session, invite volunteers to share something from **HomeBuilders Project #8.**

1. Share one thing you learned while working through *HomeBuilders Project #8.*

    _____

2. One common complaint non-Christians often raise about Christians is, "Too many Christians are hypocrites." Do you agree with that statement? Why or why not?

    _____

3. Complete the following sentence: A Christian is not a hypocrite when he or she...

    _____

    Answer: ...lives out his or her beliefs. The purpose of questions 2 and 3 is to point out the fact that many Christians do not live what they believe. People like these profess a faith in Christ, but their everyday actions reveal that their core values come from their surrounding culture or their own selfish desires.

(30-40 Minutes)

The purpose of this **Blueprints** *section is for couples to realize God's desire for them to become disciples and to commit their lives to following Christ.*

Tip: Call attention to the introductory Blueprints paragraph, then lead the class in responding to each of the questions in Section I.

While He lived on earth, Jesus called men and women to follow Him, to become disciples, or "learners." Christ the Lord still calls men and women to follow Him today.

I. God Wants You to Become Disciples (10 Minutes)

Students are on page 133.

A. Read the description of Jesus Christ choosing His first disciples in Matthew 4:18-22.

1. Put yourself in the place of the men mentioned in this passage. What do you think was difficult about their decision to follow Christ?

_____

Answer: They had to abandon their work and their homes. This had to be difficult, and they no doubt had many questions including how they would be supported and what would happen to their families.

2. What did they have to give up?

_____

Answer: Everything, but especially their security. They left their jobs and lost their security of knowing what life would be like from day to day because they were giving up their normal routine.

B. Who are some people you know who seem to have a fervent desire to serve Christ wholeheartedly?

_____

What is notable about the way these disciples live the Christian life?

_____

What sets them apart from other people?

_____

Tip: Describe someone you know who shows this desire to serve Christ.

C. What does it mean to follow Christ today?

_____

Answer: Following Jesus does not mean simply being an armchair observer, such as, "I follow the Dodgers (or the Cubs) by checking their place in the standings every week." Following involves leaving other pursuits and committing ourselves to following God's will for our lives no matter what He calls us to do. It means making Him the center of our lives. It means considering Him in all our decisions.

Tip: Call on a class member to read aloud HomeBuilders Principle #9.

HOMEBUILDERS PRINCIPLE #9:

God desires that we commit our lives to following Him.

Students are on page 133.

II. The Cost of Following Christ (10-15 Minutes)

Tip: Divide the class into groups of no more than five or six. Instruct each group to work together to complete the items in Section II. Allow five to seven minutes for groups to work, then call on people from different groups to share what their group concluded about each item.

Read what Christ told His disciples in Matthew 10:37-39.

A. According to this passage, what must a person do to become a disciple of Christ?

_____

Answer: To become disciples, we must change our priorities to put Christ first. This doesn't mean that we do not love our marriage partners and our children, but rather that we love Christ first of all. Disciples also should be willing to endure suffering and to lose their prestige, income, comfort, etc. as a result of serving Christ. It's important to note that these things may not happen, but disciples should be willing for them to happen if necessary. Disciples should be prepared to lose anything and everything to follow Christ.

B. What makes it difficult for a Christian to take a strong stand for Christ in today's society?

_____

Answer: As our society moves away from the former consensus that morality is based on God's Word, Christianity is increasingly stereotyped as a backward, intolerant religion. Taking a strong stand for Christ may mean facing unfair criticism and ridicule, and it certainly will mean moving out of our "comfort zone."

C. What are some things you are reluctant to give up in order to follow Christ?

_____

Tip: Be prepared to share something from your own life in answering this question. Perhaps you're reluctant to give up watching a certain television show or going to

R-rated movies. Or maybe it's a friendship that you really treasure but is drawing you away from your commitment to God.

D. In what ways have you had to sacrifice to follow Christ?

_____

Tip: If possible, tell the group about one or two ways that following Christ has cost you personally. Be honest in sharing your feelings about that cost, both regrets and joys.

III. The Benefits of Discipleship
(10-15 Minutes)

Students are on page 134.

Tip: Assign each small group one of the three passages under question A. Instruct the groups to read their passage and then decide on the answer to question A. After three or four minutes, call on people to share what they discovered from their assigned verse(s).

   A. What do the following verses say about the benefits of following Christ?
     1. Luke 18:28-30

_____

Answer: Whatever we may have given up to follow Christ will be given back to us many times over.

     2. John 8:12

_____

Answer: If we follow Christ, we will not walk in darkness, but have the light of life. In other words, we will see truth in a confusing world.

     3. John 8:31,32

_____

Answer: We will know the truth of His Word, and this truth will give us great personal freedom.

Tip: If you have time, ask, "In what ways does the truth set us free?"

   B. What are some benefits you've seen in your life as a result of following Christ?

_____

Tip: Open up a sharing time on question B by telling of a personal example from your own life. Then invite others in the group to share similarly.

HOMEBUILDERS PRINCIPLE #10:

The benefits of following Christ easily outweigh the costs.

Make a Date

Students are on page 134.

(5 Minutes)

This week, as they work on the HomeBuilders Project, couples will evaluate what things they have given up and need to give up to follow Christ, and also how God has blessed their obedience in the past.

Ask everyone to look at the Make a Date section of their handout, then agree with their mate on a time this week to complete HomeBuilders Project #9 together. Encourage couples to set aside 20-30 minutes to respond to the items individually and then discuss their answers together. Remind them to have their prayer notebook with them as they meet together.

Remind the group that at the next session you will again ask everyone to share one thing from the HomeBuilders Project as a way of encouraging one another and maintaining accountability with each other.

Make a date with your mate to meet in the next few days to complete *HomeBuilders Project #9.*

Be sure to bring your prayer notebook with you when you meet together to do the *HomeBuilders Project.*

Date	Time	Location

Recommended Reading

Encourage couples to enlarge on their understanding of discipleship by reading all or part of the following books.

Improving Your Serve, by Charles Swindoll.

This book contains instructions on how to become a servant of Christ in a busy, impersonal world. There is a great chapter on the rewards of serving.

The Cost of Discipleship, by Dietrich Bonhoeffer.

This is a classic account on following Christ by a German pastor who paid with his life for his stand against the Third Reich.

Dismiss in prayer or invite group members to volunteer brief prayers asking for a deepening of love for Jesus and a desire to obey His Word.

Invite everyone to enjoy a time of fellowship and refreshments.

SESSION 9

The Call to Discipleship

Growing together in Christ means considering both the call and the cost of discipleship.

1. Share one thing you learned while working through **HomeBuilders Project #8.**

_____

2. One common complaint non-Christians often raise about Christians is that "Too many Christians are hypocrites." Do you agree with that statement? Why or why not?

_____

3. Complete the following sentence: A Christian is not a hypocrite when he or she...

_____

While He lived on earth, Jesus called men and women to follow Him, to become disciples, or "learners." Christ the Lord still calls men and women to follow Him today.

I. God Wants You to Become Disciples

A. Read the description of Jesus Christ choosing His first disciples in Matthew 4:18-22.

    1. Put yourself in the place of the men mentioned in this passage. What do you think was difficult about their decision to follow Christ?

    _____

    2. What did they have to give up?

    _____

B. Who are some people you know who seem to have a fervent desire to serve Christ wholeheartedly?

    _____

    What is notable about the way these disciples live the Christian life?

    _____

    What sets them apart from other people?

    _____

C. What does it mean to follow Christ today?

    _____

HOMEBUILDERS PRINCIPLE #9:

God desires that we commit our lives to following Him.

II. The Cost of Following Christ

Read what Christ told His disciples in Matthew 10:37-39.

A. According to this passage, what must a person do to become a disciple of Christ?

    _____

B. What makes it difficult for a Christian to take a strong stand for Christ in today's society?

    _____

C. What are some things you are often reluctant to give up in order to follow Christ?

_____

D. In what ways have you had to sacrifice to follow Christ?

_____

III. The Benefits of Discipleship

A. What do the following verses say about the benefits of following Christ?

1. Luke 18:28-30

_____

2. John 8:12

_____

3. John 8:31,32

_____

B. What are some benefits you've seen in your life as a result of following Christ?

_____

HomeBuilders Principle #10:

The benefits of following Christ easily outweigh the costs.

Make a date with your mate to meet in the next few days to complete **HomeBuilders Project #9.**

Be sure to bring your prayer notebook with you when you meet together to do the **HomeBuilders Project.**

_____   _____   _____

Date   Time   Location

Recommended Reading

Improving Your Serve, by Charles Swindoll.

This book contains instructions on how to become a servant of Christ in a busy, impersonal world. There is a great chapter on the rewards of serving.

The Cost of Discipleship, by Dietrich Bonhoeffer.

This is a classic account on following Christ by a German pastor who paid with his life for his stand against the Third Reich.

HomeBuilders Project #9

Individually: 10-15 Minutes

1. Read through the entire Blueprints section.
2. What are some things that God has led you to give up in order to follow Christ as an individual?

   _____

   As a couple?

   _____

3. How has God blessed you as a result?

   _____

Interact as a Couple: 10-15 Minutes

1. Share your answers from the individual time.
2. Pull out your prayer notebook and update it, noting any answers to prayer or additional requests. Finish by praying through this notebook and once again committing your plans and purposes to the Lord. Look to Him to enable you to achieve success in this area of growing together in Christ.

Remember to bring your calendar to the next session so you can **Make a Date.**

SESSION 10

Becoming Disciples

OBJECTIVES

You will help your group members deepen their commitment to live as disciples of Jesus as you guide them to:

- Share experiences in which they have sought to live as Jesus' disciples; and
- Plan specific steps to take as a couple to love and serve others as Jesus' disciples.

COMMENTS

This session continues to challenge your class members to commit their entire lives to following Christ.

As leader, be sensitive to the varied levels of spiritual life among the members of your group. Without putting anyone down for not being as far along as they ought to be in the Christian life, lovingly nudge them toward a life of full commitment. Share openly about your own pilgrimage, letting people know of times you have struggled in following Jesus and the reasons why you continue seeking to be His disciple.

Growing together in Christ means becoming disciples of Jesus and dedicating your lives to serving others.

*Students are on
page 143.*

(10-15 Minutes)

*This session's **Warm Up** is intended to link the previous session to this session's continued exploration of discipleship.*

As people arrive, greet each person and engage them in a few rounds of the old word game "Hangman." The words they are to guess are: "disciple," "commitment," "servant," "faithful" and "obedient." To play the game, make a blank line on the chalkboard, flipchart or overhead for each letter in the first word they are to guess. Class members take turns guessing letters they think are in the word. When they guess correctly, write that letter in the appropriate blank. When they guess wrong, draw a part of the "gallows" and "victim." If they guess the word before the drawing is completed, the class wins that round, and you or your mate must give a definition of the word. If the drawing is completed before the word is guessed, then you complete the word and the class members give a definition.

When all the words have been guessed and defined, invite volunteers to share something they learned from HomeBuilders Project #9.

Share one thing you learned while working through *HomeBuilders Project #9.*

Blueprints

(30-40 Minutes)

This Blueprints section encourages couples to reflect on the blessings that God gives to those who are obedient to the disciplines Jesus describes in the Scriptures.

I. The Blessings of Discipleship (10 Minutes)

Students are on page 143.

Tip: Begin by sharing briefly one or two ways in which God has blessed you as a couple because you have followed Him. Then instruct the class members to list on their handout ways God has blessed them. After three or four minutes, invite volunteers to share one of the blessings from their list.

A. List at least three ways God has blessed you *as a couple* because you have followed Him.

_____

_____

_____

B. Share with the class one of the blessings you listed.

II. The Disciplines of Discipleship (20-30 Minutes)

Students are on page 144.

Tip: Divide the class into smaller groups. Assign half the groups to complete section A and the other half of the groups to section B. Allow five to seven minutes for groups to work, then ask for someone from each group to share their answers to their two questions. Ask the groups for as many practical ideas as possible in response to the A2 and B2 questions. Ask volunteers to tell what they think is significant about the HomeBuilders Principle linked with their assignment.

Jesus often talked about what it means to be a disciple. A disciple, for example, is one who reads the Word (John 8:31,32) and prays to the Father (Luke 11:1-4, 9-13). These are topics we've already discussed at length, so let's take a look at some of Jesus' teachings to see some additional disciplines of discipleship.

A. Read John 13:34,35.

1. Why do Christian couples who demonstrate love stand out so much in today's culture?

_____

Answer: Our society is very self-centered and self-absorbed; anyone who reaches out to others in love will stand out.

2. What are some specific, practical ways that you as a couple can show love to people...

   In your neighborhood?

   _____

   You know at work?

   _____

   In your church?

   _____

Tip: Encourage your class members to think creatively about services they could give to show Christ's love to the people around them. For example, offering to baby-sit or choosing to take an evening meal to different people each month are practical ways to show God's love. Conclude this discussion by reading aloud this HomeBuilders Principle:

HOMEBUILDERS PRINCIPLE #11:

Couples who become disciples of Christ grow by showing love.

B. Read Mark 10:42-45.

1. How can you apply this concept of serving within your own marriage?

_____

Answer: We can serve in our marriages by finding ways to meet our mates' needs, to help ease their burdens and to help them grow spiritually. This may mean denying our own desires at times and doing whatever we can to help our mates.

2. What are some ways you have enjoyed serving others as a couple?

_____

Tip: Be prepared to offer some of your own experiences here.

HOMEBUILDERS PRINCIPLE #12:

Couples who become disciples of Jesus Christ
grow by serving others.

Make a Date

*Students are on
page 145.*

(5 Minutes)

*Ask everyone to look at the Make a Date section of the handout, then agree with their mate
on a time this week to complete HomeBuilders Project #10 together. Encourage couples to set
aside 20-30 minutes to respond to the items individually and then discuss their answers together. Remind them to have their prayer notebook with them as they meet together.*

*Remind the group that at the next session you will ask everyone to share one thing from
the HomeBuilders Project as a way of encouraging one another and maintaining accountability with each other.*

*Tip: Instruct your group members to read the title deed and take turns signing both of
their title deed pages. Have them set a future date (six months or a year) to go back and look
at it again to remind them of their commitment.*

Make a date with your mate to meet in the next few days to complete *HomeBuilders
Project #10.*

Be sure to bring your prayer notebook with you when you meet together to do the
HomeBuilders Project.

Date	Time	Location

Encourage couples to enlarge on their understanding of discipleship by reading all or part of the following book.

Disciples Are Made, Not Born, by Walter Henrichsen.

This is a basic biblical study of the principles for growth and multiplication in discipleship.

Dismiss in prayer or invite group members to volunteer brief prayers asking for a deepening of love for Jesus and a desire to obey His Word.

Invite everyone to enjoy a time of fellowship and refreshments.

SESSION 10

Becoming Disciples

Growing together in Christ means becoming disciples of Jesus and dedicating your lives to serving others.

Share one thing you learned while working through HomeBuilders Project #9.

_____

I. The Blessings of Discipleship

A. List at least three ways God has blessed you *as a couple* because you have followed Him.

_____

_____

_____

B. Share with the class one of the blessings you listed.

II. The Disciplines of Discipleship

Jesus often talked about what it means to be a disciple. A disciple, for example, is one who reads the Word (John 8:31,32) and prays to the Father (Luke 11:1-4,9-13). These are topics we've already discussed at length, so let's take a look at some of Jesus' teachings to see some additional disciplines of discipleship.

A. Read John 13:34,35.

  1. Why do Christian couples who demonstrate love stand out so much in today's culture?

  _____

  2. What are some specific, practical ways that you as a couple can show love to people...

  In your neighborhood?

  _____

  You know at work?

  _____

  In your church?

  _____

HOMEBUILDERS PRINCIPLE #11:

Couples who become disciples of Christ grow by showing love.

B. Read Mark 10:42-45.

  1. How can you apply this concept of serving within your own marriage?

  _____

  2. What are some ways you have enjoyed serving others as a couple?

  _____

HOMEBUILDERS PRINCIPLE #12:

Couples who become disciples of Jesus Christ
grow by serving others.

Make a Date

Make a date with your mate to meet in the next few days to complete **HomeBuilders Project #10.**

Be sure to bring your prayer notebook with you when you meet together to do the **HomeBuilders Project.**

_____   _____   _____
        Date   Time   Location

Recommended Reading

Disciples Are Made, Not Born, by Walter Henrichsen.

This is a basic biblical study of the principles for growth and multiplication in discipleship.

Individually: 10-15 Minutes

1. Read through the entire **Blueprints** section.

2. What are some things you still need to give up in order to follow Christ as an individual and as a couple?

_____

3. Why is it difficult to give up those things?

_____

4. Write down three ways that you can begin following Christ by loving and serving others, both as an individual and as a couple.

_____

_____

_____

Interact as a Couple: 10-15 Minutes

1. Share your answers from the individual time.

2. Come to a consensus about three action steps you can take to begin following Christ as a couple:

   a. _____

   b. _____

   c. _____

3. Finish by committing your plans and purposes to the Lord. Look to Him to enable you to achieve success in this area of growing together in Christ.

4. Read together the title deed on the following page. If you agree with it, sign it to solidify your commitment to becoming disciples together.

Remember to bring your calendar to the next session so you can **Make a Date.**

TITLE DEED TO OUR LIVES

We, the undersigned, do hereby state before God and man that we have read and do understand the extent to which the following truths lay claim on our lives.

Whereas Jesus said to the multitudes:

"'If anyone comes to Me, and does not hate his own father and mother and wife and children and brothers and sisters, yes, and even his own life, he cannot be My disciple.

'For which one of you, when he wants to build a tower, does not first sit down and calculate the cost, to see if he has enough to complete it?

'Otherwise, when he has laid a foundation, and is not able to finish, all who observe it begin to ridicule him, saying, "This man began to build and was not able to finish."

'Or what king, when he sets out to meet another king in battle, will not first sit down and take counsel whether he is strong enough with ten thousand men to encounter the one coming against him with twenty thousand?

'Or else, while the other is far away, he sends a delegation and asks terms of peace.

'So therefore, no one of you can be My disciple who does not give up all his own possessions.

'Therefore, salt is good; but if even salt has become tasteless, with what will it be seasoned? It is useless either for the soil or for the manure pile; it is thrown out. He who has ears to hear, let him hear'" (Luke 14:26,28-35).

Whereas the apostle Paul reminds us:

"For to this end Christ died and lived again, that He might be Lord both of the dead and of the living" (Romans 14:9).

"For He [God the Father] delivered us from the domain of darkness, and transferred us to the kingdom of His beloved Son, in whom we have redemption, the forgiveness of sins.

"And He is the image of the invisible God, the first-born of all creation. For by Him all things were created, *both* in the heavens and on earth, visible and invisible, whether thrones or dominions or rulers or authorities—all things have been created by Him and for Him.

"And He is before all things, and in Him all things hold together.

"He is also head of the body, the church; and He is the beginning, the first-born from the dead; so that He Himself might come to have first place in everything" (Colossians 1:13-18).

Be it resolved that with full dependence upon the Holy Spirit who dwells within us, we hereby relinquish all rights to our lives, marriage and family transferring both ownership and authority to Jesus Christ, our Savior and Lord.

Witnessed our hand and seal this _____ day of _____ 19_____.

Husband _____

Wife _____

Witnessed by _____

_____

This document provided by FamilyLife of Campus Crusade for Christ.

SESSION 11

Making Disciples

OBJECTIVES

You will help each couple learn to reproduce themselves spiritually as you lead them to:

- Explore biblical and personal evidence that God can use them to reproduce themselves; and
- Discuss the need for Christian couples to witness in the power of the Holy Spirit.

COMMENTS

Session Eleven builds upon the challenging content of Session Ten. Here your group members will be challenged to reproduce themselves spiritually. Christians are not meant to merely be happy, contented people who keep the good news of Jesus Christ to themselves. An important part of the Christian life is ministering to others and sharing the gospel. Evangelism and discipleship are both an outgrowth and a catalyst for our growth in Christ.

Provide a stack of index cards (at least one card per person), plus extra pens or pencils for those who do not bring them. Also have ready a container such as a hat or shoe box.

Several days before this session, cut a small branch from a tree or shrub. Bring it to class with you.

Couples who grow in Christ will reproduce themselves spiritually by witnessing in the power of the Holy Spirit.

Warm-Up

(15-20 Minutes)

Students are on page 156.

After ten sessions your group members have probably gotten to know each other well. However, there is still value in taking time at the start of the session to help people reestablish their sense of belonging. This Warm Up is as important as any of the others in preparing group members to be receptive to the topic for the session.

Greet people as they arrive. Show your interest in them as individuals, not just as participants in your class. Ask about the events of their week. As always, start the session on time.

Tip: Give each person an index card. Provide pens or pencils to those who need them. Instruct everyone to complete the sentence in item 1 and write their answers on their index cards. Allow two or three minutes for people to think and write, then collect the index cards by having people put them in the container you brought.

1. **Complete this statement: One goal of a Christian marriage is...**

_____

Tip: Mix up the cards, then have several class members randomly select and read a statement. Whether or not any of the statements read touch on the purpose of reaching out to other people, comment that "This session will explore a vital purpose that many Christians overlook. We'll see that Christians are not meant to merely be happy, contented people who keep the good news of Jesus Christ to themselves. An important part of every Christian life and marriage is ministering to others and sharing the gospel. Evangelism and discipleship are both an outgrowth and a catalyst for a couple's growth together in Christ."

Tip: Ask for volunteers to share something they learned from the previous session's HomeBuilders Project.

2. **Share something that you learned during *HomeBuilders Project #10*.**

_____

Blueprints

(25-35 Minutes)

*This **Blueprints** section directs the group members to make the transition from just being disciples themselves to letting God use them in other people's lives. It is designed to help them apply the Great Commission given in Matthew 28:18-20 to their own lives.*

   Tip: Show the branch you brought to class. Ask these very obvious questions: "How alive does this branch se   to be? What would you expect as evidence that a branch like this is alive? How likely is it that this branch will ever produce new growth? What is this branch's problem?" (Obviously, the branch is rapidly becoming a dead stick. Having been cut off from the living plant, it is no longer capable of producing new growth.)

   Read aloud the opening paragraph of the Blueprints section.

As we learned in Session One, true growth in Christ comes as we abide in Him just as a branch abides in the vine. And Christ also makes it clear that as a result of abiding in Him, we will bear fruit: We will reproduce ourselves spiritually by helping others become disciples of Christ just as we have.

Students are on page 157.

I. God Can Use You! (15-20 Minutes)

Matthew 28:18-20 records Christ's final words to His disciples:

"All authority has been given to Me in heaven and on earth. Go therefore and make disciples of all the nations, baptizing them in the name of the Father and the Son and the Holy Spirit, teaching them to observe all that I commanded you; and lo, I am with you always, even to the end of the age."

These words are often called the Great Commission because they contain Christ's desire for every Christian to "make disciples of all the nations."

A. Look again at Matthew 4:18-20. In Session Nine we focused on Jesus' call to Peter, Andrew, James and John to "follow Me." Now consider another aspect of this passage.

   1. What does it mean to become "fishers of men"?

   _____

Answer: To reach out to men and women, bringing them to Christ. We need to go where the "fish" are, that is, where people are to communicate to them about Christ and share His love. We also need to do those things which attract fish. Fishers of men should look for ways to interest people in the gospel. For example, some non-Christians would accept an invitation to accompany you to your church, while others might be more interested in hearing a well-known Christian football coach explain how he came to know Christ.

> 2. Why do you think Christ chose working men such as fishermen to be His disciples?

> _____

Answer: First, it may have been that Christ wanted His followers to put truth into action, not to just think or philosophize about it. Second, by including ordinary working people among His disciples rather than those who were rich or powerful, He demonstrated that human hierarchies are reversed in the kingdom of God. Jesus will use anyone who is willing to follow Him.

Tip: Ask everyone to stand and find two or three partners. Then instruct the groups to spend the next two minutes discussing question B on the handout. After the two minutes are up, have people return to their seats. Invite volunteers to share with the class some of the answers they discussed.

> B. Why do many Christians think God cannot use them to influence others for Christ?

> _____

> What are some typical fears or excuses?

> _____

Answer: Most commonly, people fail to witness because they feel inadequate. Sometimes they feel this way because they have had no training in discipleship or evangelism. Often it's because they lack self-confidence and they fear rejection. Such feelings make it difficult to imagine God actually using them to do something truly significant.

Tip: Share an incident when God used you, as an individual or as a couple, to influence someone for Christ. Invite group members to share similar experiences as indicated in questions C and D. If the group is thin on such accounts, stress that the rest of the session will be helpful in equipping couples to work together as witnesses for Christ. If group members have been used in witnessing, point out that these experiences support the promises of Scripture that God will use anyone who is willing to be used. Then lead the class in silently reading HomeBuilders Principle #13.

C. How have you seen God use you to influence others for Christ...

As an individual?

_____

As a couple?

_____

D. How did your own faith grow as a result of seeing God use you?

_____

HOMEBUILDERS PRINCIPLE #13:

God can use anyone who makes himself or herself available to His call.

Students are on page 157.

II. Making Disciples Begins with Witnessing (10-15 Minutes)

Tip: Ask a class member to read aloud Matthew 9:36,37. Then lead the class in responding to the questions in Sections A-D.

A. Read Matthew 9:36,37.

    1. What do you think Christ meant when He said the "harvest is plentiful"?

_____

Answer: He and the disciples were surrounded by people who not only needed Christ, but were also ready to receive Him. These were people who were ready to be "reaped" for the kingdom of God.

    2. How is the harvest still plentiful today?

_____

Answer: We are surrounded in this world by literally billions of people who do not know Christ, yet who have great needs in their lives that can be met by Christ and His church. In our culture, there are even more pressures and temptations to cause distress than there were in Jesus' day. The need has never been greater. We have great opportunity today to become harvesters for our Savior.

Tip: Have group members think of people they know in their neighborhoods or at work. Have them describe some of these people, their problems and their needs.

B. Why do you think so few Christians regularly tell others how they can know Christ as their Savior?

_____

Answer: They are untrained, unmotivated, fearful and have not built a relationship with non-Christians. Again, the major reason tends to be a sense of inadequacy "Who am I to try to convince someone?"

C. According to John 16:7,8, who is ultimately responsible for convincing men and women that they need Christ?

_____

Answer: This is the work of the Holy Spirit. The Holy Spirit is the one who convicts people of sin.

D. What then is your responsibility in this process?

_____

Answer: Being faithful to tell others about Christ.

Tip: Before you read the following HomeBuilders Principle, be sure the people in your group understand the distinction between a Christian's responsibility in witnessing and the Holy Spirit's responsibility to bring conviction. Many people become discouraged after they explain the gospel to people who do not respond. They need to realize that only God can move hearts and that their efforts may plant a seed in someone's heart that God will use at a later date to bring the person to a decision.

HOMEBUILDERS PRINCIPLE #14:

"Successful witnessing is simply sharing the gospel in the power of the Holy Spirit and leaving the results to God." Bill Bright

Tip: Tell about a situation in which you had an opportunity to explain the gospel to someone. Tell only about the indicators you noticed that made you feel like the gospel should be shared. Do not tell whether you took advantage of the opportunity or not. Invite group members to share similar incidents from their experiences. If they find it difficult to think of appropriate situations, invite them to think of times they now recognize as potential opportunities, but may not have done so at the time.

E. If you can, share an experience in which God wanted to use you to explain the gospel to someone.

_____

Tip: After several participants have shared, ask for a show of hands of those who recall missing an opportunity, looking back and realizing that they could have said something, but simply did not do so. (This will probably include everyone.) Then invite the class to brainstorm responses to questions F and G. Be prepared to share ideas of your own.

F. What would make you more effective in your witness...
    As an individual?

    _____

    As a couple?

    _____

Answer: We can become more effective witnesses by praying specifically for God to use us at work or in activities we don't share with our spouse and to use us together with our mates. We can pray for sensitivity to opportunities which God may give us and for the discernment to know what to say and when to say it. Also, reading books on the subject of witnessing might give some new ideas for sharing the gospel with someone.

G. What opportunities can you pursue especially through your church to help you become involved in evangelism?

    _____

Answer: Many churches provide a course in personal evangelism and several Christian organizations, such as Billy Graham's, have schools of evangelism. Christian bookstores offer books and materials on witnessing. Campus Crusade for Christ offers a video curriculum, "Reaching Your World for Christ," which is among the best resources available for helping people become involved in evangelism.

Make a Date

Students are on page 158.

This **HomeBuilders Project** will help couples begin to improve their reaching out to others with the gospel of Jesus Christ.

Ask everyone to look at the *Make a Date* section of the personal study guide, then agree with their mate on a time this week to complete HomeBuilders Project #11 together.

Make a date with your mate to meet in the next few days to complete your next *HomeBuilders Project*

_____   _____   _____
Date   Time   Location

Urge participants to make a habit of reading helpful material about marriage and Christian growth. The following books will help deepen their understanding of evangelism and provide practical help for discipling others.

Witnessing Without Fear, by Bill Bright.

Here is practical training to equip the reader for evangelism and discipleship by the man greatly used of God to introduce thousands to the Savior.

Personal Disciplemaking, by Christopher B. Adsit.

This is a comprehensive, yet practical, guidebook for building a Christian from new birth to maturity.

Dismiss in prayer or invite individuals to offer brief prayers asking God's help in working as couples to make disciples.

Invite everyone to enjoy a time of fellowship and refreshments.

Making Disciples

Focus

Couples who grow in Christ will reproduce themselves spiritually by witnessing in the power of the Holy Spirit.

Warm-Up

1. Complete this statement: "One goal of a Christian marriage is..."

_____

2. Share something that you learned during HomeBuilders Project #10.

_____

Blueprints

As we learned in Session One, true growth in Christ comes as we abide in Him just as a branch abides in the vine. And Christ also makes it clear that as a result of abiding in Him, we will bear fruit: We will reproduce ourselves spiritually by helping others become disciples of Christ just as we have.

I. God Can Use You!

Matthew 28:18-20 records Christ's final words to His disciples:

"'All authority has been given to Me in heaven and on earth. Go therefore and make disciples of all the nations, baptizing them in the name of the Father and the Son and the Holy Spirit, teaching them to observe all that I commanded you; and lo, I am with you always, even to the end of the age.'"

These words are often called the Great Commission because they contain Christ's desire for every Christian to "make disciples of all the nations."

A. Look again at Matthew 4:18-20, where in Session Nine we focused on Jesus' call to Peter, Andrew, James and John to "follow Me." Now consider another aspect of this passage.

1. What does it mean to become "fishers of men"?

_____

2. Why do you think Christ chose working men such as fishermen to be His disciples?

_____

B. Why do many Christians think God cannot use them to influence others for Christ?

_____

What are some typical fears or excuses?

_____

C. How have you seen God use you to influence others for Christ...
As an individual?

_____

As a couple?

_____

D. How did your own faith grow as a result of seeing God use you?

_____

HOMEBUILDERS PRINCIPLE #13:

God can use anyone who makes himself or herself available to His call.

II. Making Disciples Begins with Witnessing

A. Read Matthew 9:36,37.

1. What do you think Christ meant when He said the "harvest is plentiful"?

_____

2. How is the harvest still plentiful today?

_____

B. Why do you think so few Christians regularly tell others how they can know Christ as their Savior?

_____

C. According to John 16:7,8, who is ultimately responsible for convincing men and women that they need Christ?

_____

D. What then is your responsibility in this process?

_____

HOMEBUILDERS PRINCIPLE #14:

"Successful witnessing is simply sharing the gospel in the power of the Holy Spirit and leaving the results to God." Bill Bright

E. If you can, share an experience in which God wanted to use you to explain the gospel to someone.

_____

F. What would make you more effective in your witness...
As an individual?

_____

As a couple?

_____

G. What opportunities can you pursue especially through your church to help you become involved in evangelism?

_____

Make a Date

Make a date with your mate to meet in the next few days to complete your next HomeBuilders Project.

_____   _____   _____
Date   Time   Location

Recommended Reading

Witnessing Without Fear, by Bill Bright.

Here is practical training to equip the reader for evangelism and discipleship by the man greatly used of God to introduce thousands to the Savior.

Personal Disciplemaking, by Christopher B. Adsit.

This is a comprehensive, yet practical, guidebook for building a Christian from new birth to maturity.

Individually: 15 Minutes

1. Look over the entire **Blueprints** section. What points were most significant to you?

_____

2. What is keeping you from being used by God to influence others for Christ?

_____

3. What is one way you've seen your mate grow as a result of this study? (Be specific and explain.)

_____

Interact as a Couple: 15 Minutes

1. Take some time to share with each other what you thought of and wrote down during the individual time.

2. What is keeping you as a couple from being used by God to influence others for Christ?

_____

3. What steps should you take to correct this situation?

_____

4. Now that this study is almost over, what steps can you take as an individual and as a couple to continue your process of growth in Christ?

_____

5. Spend some time in prayer requesting that God will use you as a couple to be key persons in the lives of your family and friends.

Remember to bring your calendar to the next session so you can **Make a Date.**

SESSION 12

Multiplying Disciples

OBJECTIVES

You will help each couple learn to build a legacy of changed lives as you lead them to:

- Identify specific people they want to see receive Christ; and
- Consider opportunities for becoming more effective in explaining the gospel to others.

COMMENTS

Tragically, only a small percentage of Christians become consistently effective witnesses. The reason Christians do not witness is often because of a sense of inadequacy. This session focuses on the very real provision God has made to provide His people with the resources needed to reproduce themselves spiritually. As the leader, you will help your group members learn to depend on the faithful presence of the Holy Spirit in their day-to-day opportunities for sharing Christ.

**Couples who witness in the power of the Holy Spirit
build a legacy of changed lives.**

Students are on page 167.

Warm-Up

(10-15 Minutes)

Even though this is the final session of this course, there is still value in taking time at the start of the session to help people continue to establish their sense of belonging. This **Warm Up** *is as important as any of the others in preparing group members to be receptive to the topic for the session.*

Greet people as they arrive. Share your appreciation for people's participation in earlier sessions.

Comment to a few couples that time has flown and that you are already down to the last session. Begin now to plant anticipation for another study sometime in the future.

As always, start the session on time.

1. Share something that you learned during *HomeBuilders Project #11.*

   _____

2. Name someone who has made an important contribution to your Christian life. What did this person do to make such an impact?

   _____

   Answer: Each person will have his own answer to this question, but hopefully one theme will emerge: Many people point to the discipling, teaching or friendship of another Christian as a key ingredient to their spiritual growth. We not only need to know how to grow, but we also need to have growth modeled for us.

   Tip: As your group members are thinking of their answers to question 3, begin by sharing about someone who has made a significant input to your own life. After several people have shared, comment on the various answers in a way that points to the theme mentioned above.

3. What one thing in your life do you most want to be remembered for?

   _____

   Answer: A theme which should emerge is that when we talk about what is most important, most people want to be remembered for who they are and the impact they have in the lives of others.

Tip: As a twist, try calling on each person to tell one thing they think people will remember about their mate. These comments may be humorous or serious. After each person has shared about his or her mate, instruct everyone to write a statement describing the one thing they most want to be remembered for. Allow a few moments for thinking and writing, then invite volunteers to share what they wrote about themselves.

Conclude this **Warm Up** with a comment such as "While there are many positive things people may remember about each of us, today we are focusing on one special legacy that each of us as couples can leave. We are going to discover how an eternal heritage can be passed on to the people we introduce to Jesus Christ."

(30-40 Minutes)

I. People Who Need Life in Christ
(10-15 Minutes)

Students are on page 168.

This exercise allows couples or individuals to begin identifying specific people they want to see receive Christ.

Make a list of 5 to 10 people you know who you want to see receive Christ. Then spend a few minutes praying specifically for each person on your list.

1. _____
2. _____
3. _____
4. _____
5. _____
6. _____
7. _____
8. _____
9. _____
10. _____

Tip: Stress the importance of identifying people they both know. Doing this will make it more likely that they can support each other in their efforts to share the good news.

Signal when two minutes are left and encourage couples to pray together about the people on their list. Individuals who have worked alone may join with a partner for prayer.

Students are on page 168.

II. The Reproduction Process (10-15 Minutes)

Comment: "The purpose of this segment is for us to discover how the spiritual reproduction process can happen just as it did for Paul and Timothy." Read aloud 2 Timothy 2:2 and the paragraph on the handout. Then lead the class in responding to questions A–C.

Read 2 Timothy 2:2. This passage describes a process of discipleship and multiplication. One person teaches another about the things of God and that person teaches another who teaches another, and so on.

A. In what ways have you seen God use you and your mate together to help others grow in their faith?

_____

B. Once you finish this study, what opportunities can you pursue as individuals and as a couple to learn more about how you can mature in your faith?

_____

C. What opportunities can you begin pursuing as individuals and as a couple to help others grow in their faith?

_____

Tip: These last two questions provide an opportunity for you as group leader to point your group members toward some practical resources available to them. Perhaps you would like to form a discipleship group of your own, or perhaps you can take the initiative to find some people in your church who can help disciple couples in your group. This also is an opportunity to build in some follow-through for the period after the study—a way of holding group members accountable for pursuing the opportunities in which they were interested.

HomeBuilders Principle #15:

Growing couples who reproduce themselves spiritually will leave an untold impact upon the next generation.

III. Your Most Important Disciples
(10 Minutes—Optional)

Students are on page 169.

Tip: If at least some of your class members are parents, be sure to reserve enough time to lead the class in responding to questions A and B.

A. Read 2 Timothy 3:14,15. How do you think Timothy's childhood instruction shaped him for his future ministry?

_____

Answer: It gave him a familiarity with the Scripture and therefore wisdom in his own salvation. It gave him a readiness to serve God, provided a healthy environment for growth and instilled the expectation that he would become like those adults in his life who taught him about Christ.

B. Why are your children your most important disciples?

_____

Answer: They are our primary responsibility and we have a greater influence on them than on anyone else. Our children are around us so much that they learn not only from our words but also from our personal example. They absorb our attitudes, our mannerisms, our weaknesses and our strengths.

Tip: Ask a class member to read aloud paragraph C. Instruct each person to make a list of his or her personal qualities that they would like to see their own children possess when they are adults. Allow several moments, then invite volunteers to share what they wrote.

C. Whether you realize it or not, you may have inherited more from your parents than physical traits. You probably absorbed many of their attitudes, weaknesses, strengths and habits. In the same way, your children will probably grow up to be much like you.

1. In what ways would you like your children to be like you when they are grown?

_____

Tip: Repeat the above process with question 2.

2. What attributes do you hope they don't inherit from you?

_____

Tip: Ask everyone to consider the answers they have written, then to write a one-sentence statement for question D.

D. What is one step you need to take to help make a better spiritual impact on your children?

_____

Students are on page 169.

This last HomeBuilders Project will help couples improve their reaching out to others with the gospel of Jesus Christ.

Ask everyone to look at the Make a Date section of the handout, then agree with their mate on a time this week to complete HomeBuilders Project #12 together.

Make a date with your mate to meet in the next few days to complete your last HomeBuilders Project in this study.

_____   _____   _____
Date   Time   Location

The following book will help deepen their understanding of evangelism and provide practical help for discipling others.

Master Plan of Evangelism, by Robert Coleman.

This is the classic work on the strategy Jesus followed in selecting and building the 12 apostles.

Dismiss in prayer or invite individuals to offer brief prayers asking God's help in working as couples to make disciples.

Invite everyone to enjoy a time of fellowship and refreshments.

SESSION 12

Multiplying Disciples

Couples who witness in the power of the Holy Spirit build a legacy of changed lives.

1. Share something that you learned during **HomeBuilders Project #11**.

    _____

2. Name someone who has made an important contribution to your Christian life. What did this person do to make such an impact?

    _____

3. What one thing in your life do you most want to be remembered for?

    _____

I. People Who Need Life in Christ

Make a list of 5 to 10 people you know who you want to see receive Christ. Then spend a few minutes praying specifically for each person on your list.

1. _____
2. _____
3. _____
4. _____
5. _____
6. _____
7. _____
8. _____
9. _____
10. _____

II. The Reproduction Process

Read 2 Timothy 2:2. This passage describes a process of discipleship and multiplication. One person teaches another about the things of God and that person teaches another who teaches another, and so on.

A. In what ways have you seen God use you and your mate together to help others grow in their faith?

_____

B. Once you finish this study, what opportunities can you pursue as individuals and as a couple to learn more about how you can mature in your faith?

_____

C. What opportunities can you begin pursuing as individuals and as a couple to help others grow in their faith?

_____

HOMEBUILDERS PRINCIPLE #15:

Growing couples who reproduce themselves spiritually will leave an untold impact upon the next generation.

III. Your Most Important Disciples

A. Read 2 Timothy 3:14,15. How do you think Timothy's childhood instruction shaped him for his future ministry?

_____

B. Why are your children your most important disciples?

_____

C. Whether you realize it or not, you may have inherited more from your parents than physical traits. You probably absorbed many of their attitudes, weaknesses, strengths and habits. In the same way, your children will probably grow up to be much like you.

  1. In what ways would you like your children to be like you when they are grown?

_____

  2. What attributes do you hope they don't inherit from you?

_____

D. What is one step you need to take to help make a better spiritual impact on your children?

_____

Make a date with your mate to meet in the next few days to complete your last **HomeBuilders Project** in this study.

Date	Time	Location

Master Plan of Evangelism, by Robert Coleman.

This is the classic work on the strategy Jesus followed in selecting and building the 12 apostles.

HomeBuilders Project #12

Individually: 15 Minutes

1. Look over the entire **Blueprints** section. What two or three points were most significant to you?

   _____

2. What steps can you take to start getting involved in discipleship and evangelism?

   _____

Interact as a Couple: 15 Minutes

1. Take some time to share with each other what you thought of and wrote down during the individual time.

2. Look at the names of people you wrote down during the session.

   a. Are there any others you would like to add to the list?

   _____

   b. Pray for each person on the list by name with both of you alternating in offering these prayers. Specifically ask God to use you in sharing the gospel with each person.

   c. Select one individual or couple on the list whom you feel is probably most receptive to you and to the gospel at this time.

   d. What common interests do you share with this person or couple?

   _____

   e. What needs do you see in the life of this person or couple?

   _____

   f. Plan a specific action or actions you will take in the next two weeks to spend some time with this person or couple.

   _____

   g. Talk together about how and when you want to share what Jesus Christ has done in your life and marriage with the person or couple you have selected.

   h. Identify the areas in which you feel you need the most help in sharing the gospel with this friend:

   ____   Introducing Christ into a conversation;

   ____   Sharing my personal testimony;

   ____   Explaining the gospel;

   ____   Guiding my friend to make a decision;

   ____   Other: _____.

i. Finally, decide together what you can do to get the help you need and feel prepared to share the gospel with this person or couple.

_____

3. If you have children, think of the spiritual legacy you want to leave them.
   a. What kind of Christians would you like them to be when they become adults?

   _____

   b. What can you begin doing over the next six months, one year and five years to build these qualities into their lives?

   _____

4. Complete this statement together: "When we die, we want to be remembered as a couple who...."

   _____

5. Spend some time in prayer requesting that God will use you as a couple to be key persons in the lives of your family and friends.

The Four Spiritual Laws*

Just as there are physical laws that govern the physical universe, so are there spiritual laws that govern your relationship with God.

Law One: God loves you and offers a wonderful plan for your life.

God's Love

"For God so loved the world, that He gave His only begotten Son, that whoever believes in Him should not perish, but have eternal life" (John 3:16).

God's Plan

(Christ speaking) "I came that they might have life, and might have it abundantly" (that it might be full and meaningful) (John 10:10).

Why is it that most people are not experiencing the abundant life? Because...

Law Two: Man is sinful and separated from God. Therefore, he cannot know and experience God's love and plan for his life.

Man Is Sinful

"For all have sinned and fall short of the glory of God" (Romans 3:23).

Man was created to have fellowship with God; but, because of his stubborn self-will, chose to go his own independent way, and fellowship with God was broken. This self-will, characterized by an attitude of active rebellion or passive indifference, is evidence of what the Bible calls sin.

Man Is Separated

"For the wages of sin is death" (spiritual separation from God) (Romans 6:23).

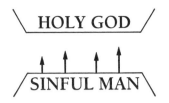

This diagram illustrates that God is holy and man is sinful. A great gulf separates the two. The arrows illustrate that man is continually trying to reach God and the abundant life through his own efforts, such as a good life, philosophy, or religion.

The third law explains the only way to bridge this gulf...

> **Law Three: Jesus Christ is God's only provision for man's sin. Through Him you can know and experience God's love and plan for your life.**

He Died in Our Place

"But God demonstrates His own love toward us, in that while we were yet sinners, Christ died for us" (Romans 5:8).

He Rose from the Dead

"Christ died for our sins . . . He was buried . . . He was raised on the third day according to the Scriptures . . . He appeared to [Peter], then to the twelve. After that He appeared to more than five hundred . . ." (1 Corinthians 15:3-6).

He Is the Only Way to God

"Jesus said to him, 'I am the way, and the truth, and the life; no one comes to the Father, but through Me'" (John 14:6).

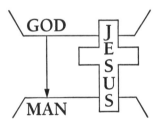

This diagram illustrates that God has bridged the gulf that separates us from Him by sending His Son, Jesus Christ, to die on the cross in our place to pay the penalty for our sins. It is not enough just to know these three laws...

> **Law Four: We must individually receive Jesus Christ as Savior and Lord; then we can know and experience God's love and plan for our lives.**

We Must Receive Christ

"But as many as received Him, to them He gave the right to become children of God, even to those who believe in His name" (John 1:12).

We Receive Christ Through Faith

"For by grace you have been saved through faith; and that not of yourselves, it is the gift of God; not as a result of works, that no one should boast" (Ephesians 2:8,9).

When We Receive Christ, We Experience a New Birth

(Read John 3:1-8.)

We Receive Christ by Personal Invitation

(Christ is speaking) "Behold, I stand at the door and knock; if any one hears My voice and opens the door, I will come in to him" (Revelation 3:20).

Receiving Christ involves turning to God from self (repentance) and trusting Christ to come into our lives to forgive our sins and to make us the kind of people He wants us to be. Just to agree intellectually that Jesus Christ is the Son of God and that He died on the cross for our sins is not enough. Nor is it enough to have an emotional experience. We receive Jesus Christ by faith, as an act of the will.

These two circles represent two kinds of lives:

SELF-DIRECTED LIFE
S - Self is on the throne
† - Christ is outside of the life
• - Interests are directed by self, often resulting in discord and frustration

CHRIST-DIRECTED LIFE
† - Christ is in the life and on the throne
S - Self is yielding to Christ
• - Interests are directed by Christ, resulting in harmony with God's plan

Which circle best represents your life?

Which circle would you like to have represent your life?

The following explains how you can receive Christ:

You Can Receive Christ Right Now by Faith Through Prayer

(Prayer is talking with God.)

God knows your heart and is not so concerned with your words as He is with the attitude of your heart. The following is a suggested prayer:

> *Lord Jesus, I need You. Thank You for dying on the cross for my sins. I open the door of my life and receive You as my Savior and Lord. Thank You for forgiving my sins and giving me eternal life. Make me the kind of person You want me to be.*

Does this prayer express the desire of your heart?

If it does, pray this prayer right now, and Christ will come into your life, as He promised.

*Written by Bill Bright. Copyright © Campus Crusade for Christ, Inc., 1965. All rights reserved.

APPENDIX B

Have You Made the Wonderful Discovery of the Spirit-Filled Life?*

Every day can be an exciting adventure for the Christian who knows the reality of being filled with the Holy Spirit and who lives constantly, moment by moment, under His gracious control.

The Bible tells us that there are three kinds of people:

1. NATURAL MAN (one who has not received Christ)
"But a natural man does not accept the things of the Spirit of God; for they are foolishness to him, and he cannot understand them, because they are spiritually appraised" (1 Corinthians 2:14).

SELF-DIRECTED LIFE
S - Self is on the throne
† - Christ is outside of the life
• - Interests are directed by self, often resulting in discord and frustration

2. SPIRITUAL MAN (one who is controlled and empowered by the Holy Spirit)
"But he who is spiritual appraises all things..." (1 Corinthians 2:15).

CHRIST-DIRECTED LIFE
† - Christ is on the throne of the life
S - Ego or self is dethroned
• - Interests are under control of infinite God, resulting in harmony with God's plan

3. CARNAL MAN (one who has received Christ, but who lives in defeat because he trusts in his own efforts to live the Christian life)

SELF-DIRECTED LIFE
S - Ego or finite self is on the throne
† - Christ is dethroned
• - Interests controlled by self, often resulting in discord and frustration

"And I, brethren, could not speak to you as to spiritual men, but as to carnal men, as to babes in Christ. I gave you milk to drink, not solid food; for you were not yet able to receive it. Indeed, even now you are not yet able, for you are still carnal. For since there is jealousy and strife among you, are you not fleshly, and are you not walking like mere men?" (1 Corinthians 3:1-3).

A. God Has Provided for Us an Abundant and Fruitful Christian Life.

Jesus said, "I came that they might have life, and might have it abundantly" (John 10:10).

"I am the vine, you are the branches; he who abides in Me, and I in him, he bears much fruit; for apart from Me you can do nothing" (John 15:5).

"But the fruit of the Spirit is love, joy, peace, patience, kindness, goodness, faithfulness, gentleness, self-control; against such things there is no law" (Galatians 5:22,23).

"But you shall receive power when the Holy Spirit has come upon you; and you shall be My witnesses both in Jerusalem, and in all Judea and Samaria, and even to the remotest part of the earth" (Acts 1:8).

THE SPIRITUAL MAN

Some Personal Traits That Result from Trusting God:

Christ-centered
Empowered by the Holy Spirit
Introduces others to Christ
Effective prayer life
Understands God's Word
Trusts God
Obeys God

Love
Joy
Peace
Patience
Kindness
Goodness
Faithfulness

The degree to which these traits are manifested in the life depends upon the extent to which the Christian trusts the Lord with every detail of his, life, and upon his maturity in Christ. One who is only beginning to understand the ministry of the Holy

Spirit should not be discouraged if he is not as fruitful as more mature Christians who have known and experienced this truth for a longer period.

Why is it that most Christians are not experiencing the abundant life?

B. Carnal Christians Cannot Experience the Abundant and Fruitful Christian Life.

The carnal man trusts in his own efforts to live the Christian life:

1. He is either uninformed about, or has forgotten, God's love, forgiveness and power (Romans 5:8-10; Hebrews 10:1-25; 1 John 1; 2:1-3; 2 Peter 1:9; Acts 1:8).

2. He has an up-and-down spiritual experience.

3. He cannot understand himself—he wants to do what is right, but cannot.

4. He fails to draw upon the power of the Holy Spirit to live the Christian life. (1 Corinthians 3:1-3; Romans 7:15-24; 8:7; Galatians 5:16-18)

THE CARNAL MAN

Some or all of the following traits may characterize the Christian who does not fully trust God:

Ignorance of his spiritual heritage
Unbelief
Disobedience
Loss of love for God and for others
Poor prayer life
No desire for Bible study

Legalistic attitude
Discouragement
Impure thoughts
Jealousy
Guilt
Critical Spirit
Worry
Frustration
Aimlessness

(The individual who professes to be a Christian but who continues to practice sin should realize that he may not be a Christian at all, according to 1 John 2:3; 3:6,9; Ephesians 5:5.)

The third truth gives us the only solution to this problem...

C. Jesus Promised the Abundant and Fruitful Life as the Result of Being Filled (Controlled and Empowered) by the Holy Spirit.

The Spirit-filled life is the Christ-controlled life by which Christ lives His life in and through us in the power of the Holy Spirit (John 15).

1. One becomes a Christian through the ministry of the Holy Spirit, according to John 3:1-8. From the moment of spiritual birth, the Christian is indwelt by the Holy Spirit at all times (John 1:12; Colossians 2:9,10; John 14:16,17). Though all Christians are indwelt by the Holy Spirit, not all Christians are filled (controlled and empowered) by the Holy Spirit.

2. The Holy Spirit is the source of the overflowing life (John 7:37-39).

3. The Holy Spirit came to glorify Christ (John 16:1-5). When one is filled with the Holy Spirit, he is a true disciple of Christ.

4. In His last command before His Ascension, Christ promised the power of the Holy Spirit to enable us to be witnesses for Him (Acts 1:1-9).

How, then, can one be filled with the Holy Spirit?

D. We Are Filled (Controlled and Empowered) by the Holy Spirit by Faith; Then We Can Experience the Abundant and Fruitful Life that Christ Promised to Each Christian.

You can appropriate the filling of the Holy Spirit *right now* if you:

1. Sincerely desire to be controlled and empowered by the Holy Spirit (Matthew 5:6; John 7:37-39).

2. Confess your sins.

By faith thank God that He has forgiven all of your sins—past, present, and future—because Christ died for you (Colossians 2:13-15; 1 John 1; 2:1-3; Hebrews 10:1-17).

3. By faith claim the fullness of the Holy Spirit, according to:

a. HIS COMMAND—Be filled with the Spirit. "And do not get drunk with wine, for that is dissipation, but be filled with the Spirit" (Ephesians 5:18).

b. HIS PROMISE—He will always answer when we pray according to His will. "And this is the confidence which we have before Him, that, if we ask anything according to His will, He hears us. And if we know that He hears us in whatever we ask, we know that we have the requests which we have asked from Him" (1 John 5:14,15).

Faith can be expressed through prayer...

How to Pray in Faith to Be Filled with the Holy Spirit

We are filled with the Holy Spirit by faith alone. However, true prayer is one way of expressing your faith. The following is a suggested prayer:

> *Dear Father, I need You. I acknowledge that I have been in control of my life; and that, as a result, I have sinned against You. I thank You that You have forgiven my sins through Christ's death on the cross for me. I now invite Christ to again take control of the throne of my life. Fill me with the Holy Spirit as You commanded me to be filled, and as You promised in your Word that You would do if I asked in faith. I pray this in the name of Jesus. As an expression of my faith, I now thank You for taking control of my life and for filling me with the Holy Spirit.*

Does this prayer express the desire of your heart? If so, bow in prayer and trust God to fill you with the Holy Spirit right now.

How to Know that You are Filled (Controlled and Empowered) by the Holy Spirit

Did you ask God to fill you with the Holy Spirit? Do you know that you are now filled with the Holy Spirit? On what authority? (On the trustworthiness of God Himself and His Word: Hebrews 11:6; Romans 14:22,23.)

Do not depend upon feelings. The promise of God's Word, not our feelings, is our authority. The Christian lives by faith (trust) in the trustworthiness of God Himself and His Word. This train diagram illustrates the relationship between **fact** (God and His Word), **faith** (our trust in God and His Word), and **feeling** (the result of our faith and obedience) (John 14:21).

The train will run with or without the caboose. However, it would be futile to attempt to pull the train by the caboose. In the same way, we, as Christians, do not depend upon feelings or emotions, but we place our faith (trust) in the trustworthiness of God and the promises of His Word.

How to Walk in the Spirit

Faith (trust in God and His promises) is the only means by which a Christian can live the Spirit-controlled life. As you continue to trust Christ moment by moment:

1. Your life will demonstrate more and more of the fruit of the Spirit (Galatians 5:22,23); and will be more and more conformed to the image of Christ (Romans 12:2; 2 Corinthians 3:18).
2. Your prayer life and study of God's Word will become more meaningful.
3. You will experience His power in witnessing (Acts 1:8).
4. You will be prepared for spiritual conflict against the world (1 John 2:15-17); against the flesh (Galatians 5:16,17); and against Satan (1 Peter 5:7-9; Ephesians 6:10-13).
5. You will experience His power to resist temptation and sin (1 Corinthians 10:13; Philippians 4:13; Ephesians 1:19-23; 6:10; 2 Timothy 1:7; Romans 6;1-16).

Spiritual Breathing

By faith you can continue to experience God's love and forgiveness.

If you become aware of an area of your life (an attitude or an action) that is displeasing to the Lord, even though you are walking with Him and sincerely desiring to serve Him, simply thank God that He has forgiven your sins—past, present and future—on the basis of Christ's death on the cross. Claim His love and forgiveness by faith and continue to have fellowship with Him.

If you retake the throne of your life through sin—a definite act of disobedience—breathe spiritually.

Spiritual Breathing (exhaling the impure and inhaling the pure) is an exercise in faith that enables you to continue to experience God's love and forgiveness.

1.   Exhale—confess your sin—agree with God concerning your sin and thank Him for His forgiveness of it, according to 1 John 1:9 and Hebrews 10:1-25. Confession involves repentance—a change in attitude and action.

2.   Inhale—surrender the control of your life to Christ, and appropriate (receive) the fullness of the Holy Spirit by faith. Trust that He now controls and empowers you, according to the *command* of Ephesians 5:18, and the promise of 1 John 5:14,15.

*Copyright © Campus Crusade for Christ, Inc., 1966. All rights reserved.

Spend Less for More Time Together!

Here's a coupon for $2.00 off your purchase of the bestselling couple's devotional from Dennis and Barbara Rainey, **Moments Together for Couples.**

With this beautiful and inspiring 365-day devotional you and your spouse will find yourselves spending more time together every day, enjoying each other's company. These full-length devotionals include insights for daily living, questions for discussion and prayer suggestions.

Grow closer to God and to one another, with **Moments Together for Couples.** Available at your local Christian bookstore.

Help Couples Spend More Time Together!

Here's a coupon for $2.00 off your purchase of **Moments Together for Couples Devotional Handouts**—a **reproducible** resource that allows you to provide daily devotionals to all the couples in your church, class or group—for just the cost of making photocopies!

Moments Together for Couples Devotional Handouts contains 60 weeks' worth of devotionals from the best-selling book **Moments Together for Couples,** by Dennis and Barbara Rainey. Each handout contains six daily readings that include insights for daily living, questions for discussion and prayer suggestions.

With these inspiring devotionals, couples will find themselves spending more time together every day, enjoying each other's company. Help couples grow closer to God and to one another, with **Moments Together for Couples Devotional Handouts.** Available at your local Christian bookstore.

$2 off Your Next HomeBuilders Bible Study Elective

Bring this coupon to your local Christian bookstore for $2.00 off your purchase of either the **Building Your Marriage** or **Building Teamwork in Your Marriage Bible Study Elective—reproducible** resources that make the best-selling HomeBuilders Couples Series® easy to teach in larger groups—like Sunday School classes.

With the **HomeBuilders Bible Study Elective Series** you can bring couples closer together each week and show them God's blueprint for better marriages.

Available at your local Christian bookstore.

Be a HomeBuilder in Your Community.

You've just finished one of the most important construction projects in your life—helping couples grow closer to each other and to God. But the work doesn't stop when the foundation is laid. You can continue helping couples build a solid framework for their marriages by introducing them to **The HomeBuilders Couples Series®**. Hundreds of thousands of couples across the nation have already begun to build stronger marriages in **HomeBuilders** small groups. Even first-time group leaders can lead these studies at home, comfortably and with confidence. It's a fun way for couples to get closer to each other and to God—and a great way to get to know their neighbors.

Building Your Marriage
By Dennis Rainey
Help couples get closer together than they ever imagined possible.
- Leader's Guide
  ISBN 08307.16130
- Study Guide
  ISBN 08307.16122

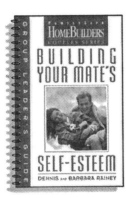

Building Your Mate's Self-Esteem
By Dennis & Barbara Rainey
Marriage is God's workshop for self-esteem.
- Leader's Guide
  ISBN 08307.16173
- Study Guide
  ISBN 08307.16165

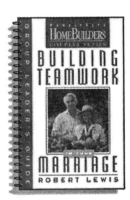

Building Teamwork in Your Marriage
By Robert Lewis
Help couples celebrate and enjoy their differences.
- Leader's Guide
  ISBN 08307.16157
- Study Guide
  ISBN 08307.16149

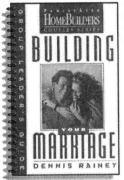

Resolving Conflict in Your Marriage
By Bob & Jan Horner
Turn conflict into love and understanding.
- Leader's Guide
  ISBN 08307.16203
- Study Guide
  ISBN 08307.16181

Mastering Money in Your Marriage
By Ron Blue
Put an end to conflicts and find out how to use money to glorify God.
- Leader's Guide
  ISBN 08307.16254
- Study Guide
  ISBN 08307.16246

Growing Together in Christ
By David Sunde
Discover how Christ is central to your marriage.
- Leader's Guide
  ISBN 08307.16297
- Study Guide
  ISBN 08307.16289

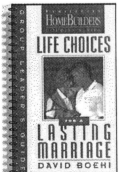

Life Choices for a Lasting Marriage
By David Boehi
Find out how to make the right choices in your marriage.
- Leader's Guide
  ISBN 08307.16262
- Study Guide
  ISBN 08307.16270

Managing Pressure in Your Marriage
By Dennis Rainey & Robert Lewis
Learn how obedience to God will take pressure off your marriage.
- Leader's Guide
  ISBN 08307.16319
- Study Guide
  ISBN 08307.16300

Expressing Love in Your Marriage
By Jerry & Sheryl Wunder and Dennis & Jill Eenigenburg
Discover God's plan for your love life by seeking God's best for your mate.
- Leader's Guide
  ISBN 08307.16661
- Study Guide
  ISBN 08307.16688

FAMILYLIFE   Look for **The HomeBuilders Couples Series®** at your local Christian bookstore.   Gospel Light

Tools for a Family Reformation.

FAMILYLIFE CONFERENCES

FamilyLife Conferences are bringing meaningful, positive change to thousands of couples and families every year. The conferences, offered throughout the country, are based on solid biblical principles and are designed to provide couples and parents–in just one weekend–with the practical skills to build and enhance their marriages and families.

A Weekend to Remember.
The FamilyLife Marriage Conference gives you the opportunity to slow down and focus on your spouse and your relationship. You will spend an insightful weekend together, doing fun couples' projects and hearing from dynamic speakers on real-life solutions for building and enhancing oneness in your marriage.

Take a Weekend to Raise Your Children for a Lifetime!
The FamilyLife Parenting Conference will equip you with the principles and tools you need to be more effective parents for a lifetime. Whether you're just getting started or in the turbulent years of adolescence, you'll learn biblical blueprints for raising your children.

☞ **To register or recieve a free brochure and schedule for these conferences, call FamilyLife at 1-800-FL-TODAY.**

FAMILYLIFE TODAY RADIO PROGRAM

Tune In to Good News for Families.
Over 1,000,000 listeners across the nation are tuning in weekly to "FamilyLife Today," recently given the **1995 National Religious Broadcasters Radio Program Producer of the Year Award**. FamilyLife executive director Dennis Rainey and cohost Bob Lepine provide a fast-paced halfhour of interviews and address practical biblical issues your family faces. So tune in this week and take advantage of this unique opportunity to be encouraged in your marriage and family.

☞ **Call 1-800-FL-TODAY for the times and stations near you.**

REAL FAMILYLIFE MAGAZINE

A New Resource for Building Families.
Our brand-new magazine, *Real FamilyLife*, is designed to communicate practical, biblical truth on marriage and family. Each monthly issue features articles, columns, and projects by Dennis and Barbara Rainey and others who will help you build a godly family.

☞ **To receive more information about FamilyLife resources, call 1-800-FL-TODAY.**

For your marriage...   for your children...
for yourself...
for a lifetime.

FAMILYLIFE
Bringing Timeless Principles Home

P.O. Box 23840 • Little Rock, AR 72221-3840
(501) 223-8663 • 1-800-999-8663
A MINISTRY OF CAMPUS CRUSADE FOR CHRIST